# STANDING UP TO BULLIES

# STANDING UP TO BULLIES

Julian L. McPhillips

NewSouth, Inc.
Montgomery

NewSouth, Inc.
105 S. Court Street
Montgomery, AL 36104
www.foranewsouth.com

CATALOGING IN PUBLICATION DATA

ISBN 978-1-961938-06-9


Printed in the United States of America

*To Laurel, Jude, Sage,*
*Nanette, Emmanuelle,*
*Julia, and Luca*

# Contents

# Preface

What a subject! Standing up to bullies is a good thing—it gives one a bully pulpit. A psychoanalytical study could be done about what makes *Bullies* like my other books. My context in this new volume draws from the legal arena, presenting true-life stories of people bullied. They are among the many people I was privileged to represent during my long legal career.

Several things suited me well for this work. First was my innate personality. As a two-year-old looking for Santa, my parents warned me: **Do not go into the living room. The boogeyman is there.** My response was, "I'll go get that boogeyman." Playing sports, especially wrestling, enhanced that quality. Our Lord Jesus's Sermon on the Mount called upon us all to look out for "the least of these our brethren." This was a foundational call to action. My legal work in the civil rights arena has enhanced this desire.

Writing is an art that I enjoy. Starting in 2005, I wrote several books on the legal world in Alabama: *The People's Lawyer* (second edition 2005) was written with co-author Carroll Dale Short; *Civil Rights in My Bones* (2016); and *Only in Alabama* (2019). In addition, I dusted off and in 2018 published *From Vacillation to Resolve,* a new version of my Princeton University honor's thesis on the French Communist WWII resistance. All these were published by NewSouth Books. This fifth work, *Standing Up to Bullies*, is a natural extension of the Covid-era years of 2020–2022, although some chapters are rooted in earlier years.

Note that any reference or insinuation by me to any person or entity as a bully is based on my opinion. I have a legal right to express such an opinion. Anyone offended who thinks I am referring to him or her, please write a rebuttal, sharing your opinion. This encourages a healthy First Amendment free-speech dialogue on the issues of the day. I certainly recognize that different opinions on almost any topic in today's world can range from A–Z. Some call this "the privilege of living in a free country." I say yes, America, but let's speak with greater civility, with as much kindness as we can. I have also been careful not to disclose any confidential attorney-client communications, and the good light in which I share their stories is well-deserved.

As to clients whose names and stories are shared herein, only certain ones were consulted. Others were not identified for their own protection, to protect them from criticism by a former employer. Again, anyone who feels wrongfully portrayed is encouraged to write his or her rebuttal and share it. Nonetheless, despite candid expressions, the author of this book expresses good will towards everyone in this book.

THE CASES-RELATED PORTION OF the book is laid out in 25 chapters:

Chapter 1, "Misty in the Midst of a Mist," portrays a Wetumpka schoolteacher in her mid-forties. She stands up to the bullying Elmore County School Board.

Chapter 2, "Getting Rheemed" is the inspiring story of an African American male in his fifties, with a tenth-grade education, who was bullied at a powerful Montgomery manufacturer.

Chapter 3, "Not Too Tall for Auburn to Bully" is an interesting, and humorous, true story.

Chapter 4, "And Thus Began the Corona Era," is one lawyer's account of the pandemic's impact on his law firm and family.

Chapter 5, "The Four Ladies of Integrity" shares the courageous story of four clients from distant parts of Alabama. She stands up to bullying treatment by the Alabama Cooperative Extension Service.

Chapter 6, "Dead Weight Takes on Her Accusers" relates to issues of human dignity.

Chapter 7 is a touching account about the lack of justice in the Lee County Sheriff's Office.

Chapter 8 is a riveting true story of a courageous Montgomerian, Mike Keller. He stood up to bully Hyundai Motor Manufacturing Company's rampant age discrimination and anti-unionism. In the end renowned U.S.

District Judge Myron Thompson compared Hyundai's lame excuses to the hapless "Wile E. Coyote" of Road Runner cartoon fame. He denied the car manufacturer's motion for summary judgment.

Chapter 9, entitled "Prosecutors can be Bullies, too," tells the hard truth about one of the worst sets of bullies.

Chapter 10 is the amazing tale of how three Selma police officers stood up to the Big Bully of an Attorney General of Alabama who indicted them, and for 3 more long years and wrongfully pursued them for the terrible felony crime of "lying to the Attorney General." What was this lie? Primarily but unbelievably, it was the so-called but untrue "misrepresentation of the condition of the Selma police evidence room." That should have been only "a difference of opinion," not a lie.

Chapter 11 involves Selma, namely the heart-warming story of Selma treasurer Ronita Wade. She was wrongfully fired three times by a bullying mayor, Dario Melton. In turn, Ms. Wade, after twice being reinstated by the Selma City Council and a third time by the Dallas County Circuit Court, obtained a federal jury verdict against the mayor, sending a statewide message.

Chapter 12 is an interesting about two different sets of African American women. They confronted institutional racism, one in the public sector against the Elmore County Board of Education. The other was in the private sector against Manpower, Inc., need we say a supplier of temporary employees to Central Alabama businesses.

Chapter 13 details how a mental health center badly bullied its older African American employees. It shouldn't have happened, but it did.

Chapter 14 tells how client Vanessa Dixon stood up to the Ku Klux Klan and on-the-job racism in Montgomery. No one else would have taken her case. We did so on a completely contingency basis. After a Montgomery federal judge ruled against her, we took her case to the 11th Circuit, U.S. Court of Appeals in Atlanta and won. This involves a courageous woman. She showed enormous gratitude to me. My law firm team helped her stand up to the Ku Klux Klan. This was, and is, music to my ears. She told us she was enormously honored to be included in this book.

Chapter 15 tells the brave story of a female employee of a powerful insurance corporation, who stood up to the corporation president's wrongful sexual harassment and retaliation. By filing a charge with the Equal Employment Opportunity Commission (EEOC), the names of the parties have been changed. That was to protect the guilty via a confidentiality agreement. The underlying facts were a painfully true story for a real person.

Chapter 16 raises the issue of who, if anyone, was the bully in the City of Montgomery's allowing multiple dilapidated apartments, if the bully were to remain in a downtown location, historically known as the "Grove Court Apartments." Built in 1947, the apartments were abandoned in the mid-1980s. They became an ugly eyesore and were a public and private nuisance. There was also a grave danger to the public from asbestos fumes if it ever caught fire. So, I represented a number of Perry Street building owners, including myself, in filing suit . . . Read this chapter, and see for yourself what happened. Then determine for yourself who was really the bully.

Chapter 17 tells the story of the vindication of a former Alabama Supreme Court chief justice and U.S. Senate candidate. He was tarred and feathered by the press. He was then bullied by an unfair defamation lawsuit against him.

Chapter 18 tells how a brave young Thomas Travis courageously took on Auburn University's Athletic Department. This subjected him to unwelcome racism. He was also wrongfully fired. Auburn made him a scapegoat for an alleged grade-changing scandal. He was not disclosing what he did not know.

Chapter 19 tells how four brave middle-aged women stood up to flagrant injustice in three Auburn University academic departments.

Chapter 20 demonstrates how the "summary judgment standard" of the law is often abused by federal courts, with the result that injured parties feel quite bullied.

Chapter 21 addresses the bullying effect of the doctrine of sovereign immunity, state action immunity, and qualified immunity protecting bad apple cops while denying civil rights justice to victims.

Chapter 22 explains how involuntary arbitration was forced so unfairly upon unwilling employees and consumers which is extremely bullying, denying many Alabamians fairness and justice.

Chapter 23 describes how Anti-Semitism, even in the workplace, is still alive and well. It also describes how one Court had a chance to do something about it but ducked the moral opportunity on an incorrect technicality.

Chapter 24 tells the outrageous story of the biggest bully of them all in Alabama, the infamous, deadly torture chambers. They are called Alabama's prisons. This is where stabbings, bludgeoning and rapes are commonplace. All inmates carry knives or other weapons, and most use illegal drugs.

Chapter 25, "Wrapping it Up" is not a summary of the other chapters but is an encouragement to readers to take on the bullies in their lives.

As in my last two law-related books, there is a travel section. It was initiated as a Covid interlude. During 2020–2021, Leslie and I traveled within the southeastern United States and California. In 2022, we returned to international travel, this time with trips to the Netherlands, Denmark, and Greenland (I wrote Chapter 25 above while in Greenland). We survived to tell the stories and hope you enjoy them.

I expect no financial gain from this book. In fact, the costs will exceed any monetary benefits. However, there is a message to impart: Stand up for yourself. Roll with the punches. The individuals whose stories have been shared will feel honored for the recognition of standing up to bullies. Their efforts should be appreciated in the Heavenly realms.

# Acknowledgments

Foremost, and overall, I remain profoundly grateful to God for the enormous blessing of life itself, good health, peace, and prosperity. This also involves good family relationships and a wonderful law practice, also a business and ministry in many ways. God has always been there, through faith and prayer, whenever I need Him. I have a law practice that moves quickly from day-to-day. I tell prospective clients I need God many times during a day, as He's accessible . . . Seek ye first the kingdom of God . . .

My next level of gratitude goes to my awesome wife and life partner, and soulmate. She is also my best friend, named Jeanne "Leslie" Burton in Brazil. She is of American parents, with my initials now as "J. Leslie McPhillips." What an inspiring job Leslie does as mother of our three grown children, Rachel, Grace, and David. Each one involves our advice and example, and each has enjoyed a happy marriage. Between them, there are seven beautiful grandchildren, Laurel, Jude, Nanette, Sage, Emmanuelle, Julia, and Luca. What a joy each has been. Thank you, Lord.

At the law firm, Amy Strickland, as office manager of 25 years, and Kenneth Shinbaum, as law partner of 36 years, have my greatest gratitude. They now work with law partner David Sawyer. This involves primarily employment cases and criminal defense. Law partners Aaron Luck, Jim Bodin, and Joe Guillot rank high in the gratitude department. There are also firm attorneys Tanika Finney and Andrea Hatchcock.

Amy has an ability to do much quickly. She is office manager, bookkeeper, computer fixer, and advertising manager, as well as HR director, PR director, Fitzgerald Museum treasurer, and manager to confidant and friend. "Amazing Amy" unquestionably deserves enormous credit for my success and the firm's.

As of January 2022, my two senior-most law partners, Kenneth at 70 and Joe at 68 stepped down as partners, semi-retired and became, of counsel. They are still able attorneys. Both also remain as good friends.

My most valuable law partner in the new partnership at the time of this writing (mid-2022) has been "of counsel," namely David Sawyer, age 58. He remains in Birmingham. His home is located there, where he works on briefs, motions, and correspondence, David frequently sends me materials for review. We stay in touch by phone three to four times each workday when we're not in court. There is a "symbiotic" nature in our work, in that we jointly interact with each other. No doubt David is brilliant academically, legally, and morally. He truly believes in Jesus's words from the Sermon on the Mount. That is, "Inasmuch as you do it for the least of these my brethren, you have done it unto me."

Kenneth Shinbaum and I continue to enjoy an interesting relationship. Given the very different views we sometimes have had about case prospects, we often complement one another. Ken's warnings have kept me out of trouble. Joe Guillot's leadership assistance on criminal cases has been especially invaluable. He has done valuable work in other fields. That includes employment law and Social Security.

Aaron Luck and Jim Bodin, both in their fifties, have both been very helpful law partners from 2006 through 2022. They have been with me since the mid 1990s. They specialize in personal injury cases, and pride themselves on "hitting the long ball." That is a metaphor for a good settlement. They usually rank number two or three in annual attorney fee production after me. They depend more on the advertising arm of the firm than do I.

Attorneys Tanika Finney, 40, and Andrea Hatchcock, 35, are two valuable attorneys. They have ably assisted the firm. Tanika has a degree of independence in her schedule, and Andrea is a full-time associate attorney. Tanika deserves double credit for helping me type this book. She made helpful suggestions along the way. Tanika has ably assisted me on several cases in this book. She has also been a true friend. On November 1, 2022, she moved on to a new daytime job with the Alabama Department of Labor but remains in touch.

My number one paralegal, Cesaire Jane McPherson, has done a stellar job! She has assisted me for the better part of two years now, 2020–2022, and was responsible for the final revisions in the completion of this book. She was also my last paralegal, following enthusiastically in the footsteps of several previous excellent paralegals. That includes Regina Barron, 1978–87; Lynelle Howard, 1987–97 and 2007–13; Bridget Strength, 2018–2020; and Denise Bertaut, in the early 2000s. The incomparable Amy Strickland (1996– ), is still ongoing). She graduated from paralegal to office manager years ago and provides incredible leadership to our firm. We call her the "mother of the firm." I am "the daddy," having founded the firm in 1978.

Great appreciation is due to our firm's long-time runner and server of process Kaylon Jenkins at 46, in his 25th year of service. Kaylon is also a professional minister, doubling humbly as the firm's chaplain.

Stephany Moore, at 29, is the youngest employee in the firm. She does an excellent job as our receptionist. Our dearest gratitude goes to Page McKee, paralegal for Aaron, having reached her 25th anniversary this year and Dana Simon, paralegal for Jim.

Ms. Wendy Newman has greatly assisted me during Covid years, but has moved on to another opportunity, in 2022. She is greatly missed.

Special gratitude goes to several outside attorneys. They have encouraged me and others in this firm in various ways. Bobby Segall, my own personal attorney, is of foremost help. Words cannot describe the depth of my gratitude to Bobby, whom I consider a saint. Tommy Gallion, a long-time friend, has an enormous sense of humor, and was a de facto law partner with me from 1978–82. He remains high on my gratitude list.

Other lawyers have inspired me, including Tommy Kirk, who is King of the DUIs. Griffin Sikes Jr. takes on tough cases against law enforcement wrongdoing. I also refer cases to Doug Ghee of Anniston, with his law firm of four daughters and three sons-in-law, and they do so back to me. Former law partners Jim DeBardelaben, Frank Hawthorne Jr., William Gill, Mary Goldthwaite, and Allen Stoner of Decatur were also enormously helpful to the firm in the years they worked for us.

Speaking of attorneys, one special one from Birmingham, now retired, whom I revere, respect, and love, is my brother Frank McPhillips, eight years younger than I am. In earlier years (the 1960s–'70s) before marriages for us both, we traveled widely in Western Europe and camped out in the Rocky Mountain West. Since the 1980s we have been next-door neighbors on frequent weekends at Lake Martin, where our children have grown up together.

Gratitude goes to many others advising me on this book. That includes Randall Williams, Suzanne La Rosa, David Sawyer, Kendra Doten, Daron Harris, Rev. Doug Carpenter, Cesaire Jane McPherson, and my wife Leslie, among others.

# STANDING UP TO BULLIES

# 1

# Misty in the Midst of a Mist

The above rhythmical phrase I can't shake from my brain; it's like music that won't quit playing in one's head. This lyrical burst of words captures it all in a nutshell. The true story of what happened to a teacher named Misty is mystifying. It is the sort of thing not shakable by a good night's sleep. What really happened? How did Misty endure it all?

Her name is "Misty Trussell." She walked into my office in April 2019. This schoolteacher was struggling at the Redland Elementary School in Wetumpka, which she helped found in 2009. This graduate of Auburn University in Montgomery spent years in elementary education. She was a role model for many teachers and inspired others. An accomplished singer, she devoted countless voluntary hours on most school mornings training a student choir. Students, parents, and fellow teachers worshipped the ground on which she walked. Misty was popular . . . a "force of nature."

Then Misty found herself in a fog-like atmosphere descending upon her. Clear thinking was interrupted, and this bullying caused her to feel she was gradually being sucked into quicksand.

Thirteen months earlier, in March 2018, Misty first came to see me. She was placed on an involuntary leave of absence by the Superintendent of Elmore County Schools. She wasn't sure what hit her, when, or why, or was exactly she was doing.

She had experienced an unfair grade audit imposed by Redland principal Chad Walls. Misty sought my help with this targeting. She was bothering no other teachers. The principal appeared very jealous of her following in the school. Walls, unlike Misty, was not a founder at Redland Elementary. He had a covetous feeling. The 10th Commandment says "thou shalt not covet." That is a human weakness most people struggle with.

An entire year passed before this earnest but worried teacher came calling again to my office in the spring of 2019. Her familiar smile kindled my memory.

This time allegations sprang from a 10-year-old boy in the fourth grade. He was claiming that Misty had hit him. She was blown away by this ridiculous charge. What was this, and who had hit whom? What nerve! She had no idea what the young man was talking about. We'll call him "C.H.," and he had a history of dreaming things up. Suddenly reports on Channel 12 TV news in Montgomery told about an unnamed teacher striking a student at Redland Elementary. Embarrassing rumors were rife that it was Misty.

Causing further heartburn, the story originated with the young boy's father's girlfriend. The accusations smacked of financial opportunity. Misty received voluminous supporting statements from many parents. They quoted their children that nothing had ever happened. The whole dilemma resembled a soupy fog. It was like steam slowly rising from a warm lake, cooling upward. It was growing thicker by the minute. Misty was bamboozled. At times she was irate and depressed.

I fired off an epistle—let's call it a missile—to the Elmore County Schools superintendent and the Redland principal demanding that Misty's suspension be lifted. She was allowed back in her classroom. A few weeks of silence ensued, broken only by occasional communications between the school board's Birmingham attorney and me. Instead of an undesirable transfer as a teacher, Misty was terminated in late May 2019. The reason given was her excessive discipline of the young boy. The superintendent's letter exaggerated her offense.

Instead, she was given the right to contest the accusations. Contest them we did, leading to a full-blown evidentiary hearing before the Elmore County School Board. Leslie's and my 45th anniversary family trip to Alaska and Canada was looming. The trial was not scheduled until July 2019.

We trimmed our witness list down from 150 to 10. This was no small challenge. Numerous prep meetings at my office were held with Misty. Her recently widowed mother, Beverly, and good friend Sandra Williford concurred. Co-counsel Tanika Finney was usually present with invaluable assistance. Leslie and I met with Misty and her husband at the Hog Rock Bar-B-Q cafe in Wetumpka en route to Lake Martin.

The day of reckoning arrived in July 2019. We appeared at the Elmore County Board of Education in Wetumpka. A spirited, all-day hearing sparked Misty's supporters. The solemn school board consisted of seven members—four older white men, an elderly black gentleman, and two white ladies. The one female board member prejudiced the proceeding, calling Misty out as a liar.

The battle was long and feisty. Despite good evidence supporting Misty, the board had made up its collective mind. Given their preexisting loyalties to the superintendent, the board quickly acquiesced to the superintendent's recommendation. It upheld Misty's termination.

I initiated follow-up negotiations. The Elmore County Board of Education reversed itself. It rehired Misty and allowed her to resign. Meanwhile, Misty found a much better special education teaching job in the private sector. She was more than ready to move on, and so were we. The mist finally lifted, and Misty succeeded. She was breathing much better. The sun rose again. To her credit, Misty had stood up to this bully. She came out swinging and was radiantly excited about her new opportunity.

## 2

# Rheemed but Redeemed

Rheem Manufacturing Company is a private manufacturer of electrical equipment. It was founded in 1974. By 2019, it had grown to 5,700 employees. Its headquarters was in Atlanta, but Montgomery has long been a primary manufacturing locale for the large corporation. Rheem's specialties were water heaters, pools and spas, home generators, heat pumps, and gas furnaces. It serves a worldwide market, hungry for its products.

This is not the first-time clients of mine have been bullied, or "rheemed" by Rheem. During the last 30 years, our firm has helped at least four–five other clients take on Rheem. One such case was famous for its aggressive handling by former partner Mary Goldthwaite, and it took years to finalize. Another great injustice involved a Rheem plant manager terrorizing my white-collar client. It resulted in a substantial settlement, in a short time.

On the bright side was Barbara Ann McGuire Cook. She was a classmate of mine from Columbia Law School, Class of 1971. She was general counsel at Rheem for years. She was a very pleasant person to work with. We frequently resolved cases amicably before they ever reached a litigation stage. It was a preferable resolution for both sides.

Rheem employee John Oliver entered my office in September 2018. A 54-year-old African American, he had a 10th-grade education. He was also a side-scene welder who had worked at Rheem for 30 years. Oliver was truly upset in coming to see me. He complained that his female supervisor, Catherine Arnold (name changed to protect the guilty), was "sexually harassing" him. She repeatedly kept asking him for money, insinuating strongly what he would get in return. She even insisted on coming over to his home at night, after work, to see him. She wanted to give him "a good time." All she wanted was money in return.

She had even gotten his private telephone number. She was repeatedly calling him from 2:30 to 3 a.m. It became so bad that Oliver's live-in girl-friend broke up with him.

Oliver asked Rheem's human resources department for help. The managers even asked Arnold to quit. She refused. This gave Oliver a legitimate claim against Rheem, for the company's inability to stop her. On October 18, 2018, we helped Oliver file a sexual harassment charge with the Equal Employment Opportunity Commission (EEOC) in Birmingham.

Rheem eventually terminated Arnold, but it turned up the pressure on Oliver, retaliating against him, and ultimately firing him in February 2019. At that time, he was on "light duty," due to an on-the-job injury. It was a job he could perform well despite his deteriorating disc, scoliosis, and a pinched nerve.

Upon being fired, Oliver had a total loss of income. He returned to my office and was highly incensed. He was seeking justice. In March 2019, we filed a supplemental EEOC charge, alleging illegal retaliation, disability, and continuing sex discrimination. This flowed from the original sexual harassment.

Oliver could perform all the necessary duties of his light-duty job. In June 2019, we obtained a "right to sue" from the EEOC. Following fruit-less negotiations, we filed suit against Rheem. Six months later, we received a "right to sue," and took it to court.

My associate attorney Chase Estes helped me put together a good discovery package. We sought important information from Rheem and the EEOC. The battle was on!

On August 16, 2019, in violation of all ethical norms, Rheem's Human Resources director Leah Price used her sneaky move to lure Oliver back to Rheem's plant without his attorney. Not knowing it was a trick, Oliver didn't tell me anything about it. Once there, Rheem pressured Oliver to sign paperwork with the promise of retirement income. The unfortunate effect was that it bolstered Rheem's defense that Oliver was not fired back in February 2019. He was simply continued on FMLA (Family Medical Leave Act), until his time ran out. That defeated our claim.

This underhanded and deceitful act by Rheem caused us to amend our federal suit in January 2020. We claimed common law fraud and violations of statutory law. Frankly, I was quite angry.

Gearing up for trial, associate attorney Chase Estes set up a mediation conference. In March 2020, we met with a federal magistrate judge, and worked it out. Typically, any final resolution is subject to a strict confidentiality provision, signed by the parties. Nothing more revealing can be shared. Notwithstanding, Oliver walked out of the federal courthouse that day. His head was high. He had stood up to the bully corporation, which had mistreated him. He felt 100 percent better, and I felt well.

# 3

# Even Giants Can Be Bullied

At 6'11" and 275 pounds, Cameron Boozer was too big to be bullied, but at Auburn University, strange things happen.

On October 16, 2017, this gentle giant called upon me. He was a 45-year-old African American from Lanett in Chambers County, near the Georgia border. He was "Mr. Alabama Basketball." He led his hometown high school team to state championships in the early 1990s. He starred as a center for the Auburn University Tigers and averaged 20 points per game. Five years of professional basketball in Europe and law enforcement experience in Georgia ensued. Boozer was then hired by Auburn University in 2012 to work in its campus safety and security department.

Boozer was a dedicated employee. He consistently achieved top personnel ratings at Auburn. Unfortunately, he had one big disadvantage. It wasn't his height. He was a black employee at the whitest school in the Southeastern conference. His difficulty in 2016 was Chance Corbett, associate director of the campus safety and security department, who had become the "interim" executive director and thus called the shots.

Given this additional authority, Corbett was a bully boy of sorts, dishing out problems by October 2017 to another black administrator, Regina Hutchinson. Belittled and ostracized, this lady experienced a "cold and hostile working environment." Corbett carried a loaded pistol in his boot. This was an implied threat. Boozer was disappointed but not surprised when Corbett passed him over for a top promotion. Boozer had applied for and deserved the position. In all fairness, this should have been Boozer's, as the new associate director.

Meanwhile, three white administrative employees achieved higher positions in 2017. This included Chance Corbett promoting himself. He was now presiding over the entire department. He enjoyed a $9,000 raise.

Susan McCallister was promoted to director of campus safety compliance, with a $7,000 raise. Robert Mann, an emergency management planner, also received a hefty raise. All three elevations came in unposted positions. That meant the private hand of Corbett enabled them to bypass competition from black employees.

Boozer did not sit idly by or take this lying down. In August 2017, he interviewed for the newly opened associate director position. This one was posted by Corbett, unlike the others.

Competing for this desirable position were three white men, all invited to the Auburn campus for "meet-and-greet" sessions with Corbett. Boozer was not invited. He was required, however, to be present, to meet the three applicants. Boozer was eventually allowed to interview with Chance Corbett over Skype, but not face-to-face. Corbett's bias towards Boozer's candidacy emerged early on.

In October 2017, Boozer learned that Corbett had chosen Tony Dean, a comparatively inexperienced white male from Faulkner University in Montgomery, to be his new associate director. Not surprisingly, it became Boozer's responsibility to train Dean in Boozer's "Campus Security Services" division. Neither Dean nor Corbett knew much about it. Boozer frequently advised Corbett about his own section of the department, but rarely ventured around it.

Auburn University has its own Equal Employment Opportunity (EEO) rule book. Before the offer could be made to Tony Dean, the rule book required it be cleared by Auburn's Affirmative Action Officer, Michelle Martin. That did not happen. The necessary step was conveniently bypassed by Corbett, and Dean received his job without a clearance.

EEO Officer Martin was upset by Corbett's statement that Boozer's "experience did not rise to the level of other applicants." Martin replied: "Would you please have someone clarify what this means . . ." Corbett conveniently ignored the request.

Boozer was understandably disappointed by Corbett's selection of the less-experienced Dean, who was less qualified by all objective yardsticks of Auburn University's policies and procedures. Boozer had significant law enforcement experience, but Dean had none.

Campus Security co-employee Regina Hutchinson, in her own filing with the E.E.O.C. in Birmingham, had months earlier said that Chance Corbett was "much more comfortable with white employees than Black employees, especially in higher-level positions." Corbett was too smart to use racial epithets. "Nonetheless, his racial discrimination in running the department was clear and obvious," said Hutchinson, based on abundant circumstantial evidence.

The denial of the Associate Director of Campus Safety position, due to his Black race, violated federal law, cost Boozer financially, and caused him great mental anguish.

Rarely is any case quickly resolved at Auburn. Boozer's case rocked along for another two and a half years. A right-to-sue letter from the EEOC was received in March 2018, allowing us to file a suit in May 2018.

Skilled Auburn defense attorney Kelly Pate peppered us with her usual tough defense. She tied us up on motions to dismiss. She raised vague issues. I needed good help, and quickly secured our firm's "of counsel" attorney Tanika Finney. She energized the case with valuable assistance in defending against Kelly's motions.

Meanwhile, I got to know Boozer much better personally. I learned that he had twin sons, both 6'9". They were hotly recruited by everyone except Auburn.

This was a different form of bullying, a type of Boozer was not used to. No one hit him over the head, not that anyone could reach that high. No one ever called him by racial names. But the continuing flow of the Caucasian demographic culture at Auburn was suffocating. Many Auburn professors admitted this was an embarrassment for this otherwise respected southern university.

It was to Boozer's credit that he stood up unflinchingly, enduring this great injustice, with its bullying aspects. Confidentiality restrictions prohibit us from sharing how well this case was resolved for Boozer. Nonetheless, in mid-January 2020, after meeting renowned mediator Phil Adams at his Opelika office, the case came to a screeching halt. A smiling Boozer emerged, feeling vindicated. He was no longer just a former Auburn basketball hero who had led the victorious Tigers. Following the mediation, he moved on with his life at a new job. He enjoyed more time with his wife. He joyfully reveled over his twin sons' spectacular success in basketball at Troy University. He joyfully became a more full-time dad to his high school daughter.

And he became a lifetime friend to me.

Ten months later, in November 2020, co-employee Regina Hutchinson's case was also favorably "resolved." She remained, however, employed at Auburn's Safety and Security department. Co-counsel Tanika Finney again assisted in engineering a good legal outcome, and Hutchinson was most satisfied.

# 4

# And Thus Invaded the Corona Bully

## 2020–2021

After hearing much from our office the week of March 9–13, 2020, Leslie and I returned on Sunday, March 15, from the Gulf Coast beaches to a Montgomery pulsating with a nationwide hysteria about the Coronavirus contagion.

During the preceding week vacationing in Mississippi, telephone calls from our office staff at the McPhillips Shinbaum law firm conveyed increasing concern about the advancing COVID bully. Everything was being super-cleaned. Church services and school days were canceled state-wide. Panic soared. Hysteria was setting in, at least in some quarters.

We didn't let that stop us from gathering that Sunday at 6 p.m. for a "Praise and Worship service" on the front porch of our Old Cloverdale home. Those gathered belted out praise and worship songs, scaring away the Coronavirus. The twelve in attendance included four African American musicians. Eight others included our Episcopal priest David Peeples, members Steve Watkins and Charise Dudley, immigrant Alice Yan of China, and an ASU professor with her two young children. Leslie and I led the service. Three races enthusiastically worshiped together. We dodged the Corona bullet and spiritually challenged that bully.

Front-porch services continued for six straight Sundays, through April 26, 2020, notwithstanding "Stay at Home" orders tanking the economy and spiking paranoia. These worship services continued the last Sunday of each month from May through the summer and fall, Christmas season, and well into late 2022, when this book was being finished. We chimed out these Holy Spirit-inspired songs. We believed we were scaring away the

Corona bully. The four musicians usually wore masks. I usually did not. I simply couldn't sing or preach that way. The mask caused me to breathe poorly or cough and muffled my voice. I could not maintain adequate social distance.

Soon, I made an amazing discovery. It was that I had a built-in protection with my O-negative blood type, which only 6 percent of people nationally have. However, I was relying upon faithfulness, combined with scientific protocol, to keep us healthy. It did so throughout the next 24 months, from March 2020 to March 2022. This chapter is limited to that time period.

Upon returning to my law office that first Monday, March 16, 2020, a different era had begun, with quite an aura! Office manager Amy quickly informed me that three law partners—Kenneth Shinbaum, Aaron Luck, and Joe Guillot—had underlying health conditions that made them more vulnerable. Only Jim Bodin and I were condition-free. Employees were scurrying around, rubbing down tables and doorknobs. The front and back doors of the building had signs warning prospective clients with symptoms to go home and call back later for appointments.

There was a big immediate impact on the family front. My dear son David was to be married at "Burritt on the Mountain," a prominent location in Huntsville, on April 5, 2020. Over 100 invitations had been sent to family and friends coming in from nine states. Given the sudden hysteria, many started canceling, and the whole wedding was postponed.

Not to be scuttled by the Corona bug, David and Melinda on a sudden inspiration Saturday, March 21, 2020, were married at our "McP Retreat" place at Lake Martin on the top deck of our dock. Leslie and I were the only guests. I did the officiating and notarizing. They now have a framed picture of the marriage certificate in their South Carolina home.

The junior-most attorneys in the firm were Chase Estes, Tanika Finney, and David Sawyer. They all worked remotely from their homes. The five partners worked at our office. David was 55 in 2020. He thus was not a junior but preferred working from his Birmingham house anyway. He was otherwise dependent on a ride to Montgomery because of an epilepsy condition preventing him from driving. Otherwise, Covid did not interfere with the brilliant scholarship of his work. With so many state employees suddenly remaining at home, he worked remotely. This evaporated David's previous daily ride to Montgomery with a state attorney from Birmingham. Instead, his college-aged son and others gave David necessary rides to Montgomery for depositions, or to Wetumpka for court hearings.

As president and senior partner of the firm, I felt strongly that more information was needed on the front and back doors of the law office building. I remembered the signs on the McPhillips Fieldhouse at St. James School. I recall the famous words of Joe Kennedy, father of JFK and RFK. They were, posted on the doors in plain view: "WHEN THE GOING GETS TOUGH, THE TOUGH GET GOING."

I didn't stop there but added another sign on the front and back doors. I encouraged all necessary scientific precautions but quoted God's words to King Solomon 3000 years ago in 2 Chronicles 7:14, during a pandemic in Biblical times:

If my people who are called by my name will humble themselves, and pray and seek my face, and turn from their wicked ways, then I will hear from heaven, and will forgive their sin and heal their land.

That first week back, starting March 16, 2020, was quizzical. What was best for us, as a firm, to do? I started a daily 8 by 11 inch devotional sheet. It was entitled "1st Day of CVC" (Corona Virus Containment) with a smaller centerpiece page. I quoted words from devotional writer Sara Young's book, *Jesus Calling*. Scriptural quotations were included. They were hand-written words of encouragement. Initially placed in employee boxes, these devotionals were later emailed to everyone.

A deep spiritual component appeared to exist within this pandemic. It was similar to the plagues of Egypt. The worst plague had led to "Passover," now widely celebrated in both Jewish and Christian circles. I reassured my staff, including ultra-cautious law partner Kenneth Shinbaum, that we were still practicing all necessary precautions in the scientific realm.

Business at the firm slowed. It was far from a crawl, or a halt. Although the streets were sparse, I was pleasantly surprised to see so many prospective clients still coming in. Our firm's reputation for successful outcomes was with the Alabama Department of Corrections. That is where cases have soared in recent years. Hence numerous new clients were flowing in from all over the state, but a significant segment of this terribly mistreated job sector sought my help.

Even two prison wardens, namely Warden III Gwendolyn Greaves and Warden II Errol Pickens, came for legal help. They became scape-goats, so named by the misguided Commissioner Jefferson Dunn. Law partner Joe Guillot ably assisted me on both cases. He also did so with the legal defense of two Bibb Correctional officers wrongfully indicted, namely Jordan Thomas and Keith Finch. All this was happening through-out March and April 2020, when almost everyone else locally, lawyers included, were "hunkering down" at home.

Our capital city was beginning to look like a ghost-town. Since I do not type, the Governor's "stay-at-home orders" didn't suit me. Fortunately, paralegals Bridgett Strength, Cesaire McPherson, Wendy Newman, and office manager Amy Strickland kept me going. Amy typed, and organized my cases for firm attorneys Tanika Finney, David Sawyer, and Chase Estes, albeit from remote locations, and kept up their productive assistance.

In early April 2020, Transportation Department (DOT) employee Carlos Thomas anxiously sought help. He was wrongfully suspended for missing a working weekend due to a genuine fear about a co-employee's family member being contagious with COVID-19. Back at home, Thom-as's wife and mother had serious immune deficiencies. Nonetheless, a live hearing occurred at the DOT on April 7, 2020, where several witnesses were masked. Others, however, did not mask, including the DOT attor-ney, the hearing officer, and me. Fortunately, my client received a good result. No one caught any virus!

Notwithstanding Corona, other clients kept streaming into the office, from April to December 2020 and into 2021 and 2022. We were mostly masked, but not all. My four partners Kenneth, Joe, Aaron, and Jim, or some combinations thereof, were at the office every day. They were usually masked when meeting with clients. I usually did not mask, despite office manager Strickland's repeated diplomatic encouragement that I do so.

Again, a mask made it difficult to breathe. It stifled my voice. In addition, I was assisted by my blood type and faith. That was while still maintaining the social distance protocol.

At home, our spiritual discipline grew stronger. I spent more time than ever on my son David's prayer kneeler. That was across the foyer from my upstairs bedroom. The kneeler has a lit-up glass cross, depicting scenes from Christ's life to inspire and strengthen faith, and it did so with me. Likewise, twice-daily prayers with dear wife Leslie became more energized and more meaningful than ever. It was "faith over fear," words repeated every Sunday by Methodist pastor Jay Cooper, in sermons we enjoyed by TV at Lake Martin on weekends. He kept saying "Exhale fear; inhale faith." We did.

Given the solemn drumbeat daily of media reports on COVID-19 deaths and infections, I felt it necessary to be covered by the Holy Spirit, to combat the anxiety. Sometimes that included hysteria, from within the office. One evening, Wednesday, May 27, just after arriving home, I received a telephone call from partners Kenneth Shinbaum and Joe Guillot. They were panicking that a substitute receptionist a week earlier had symptoms. A 4–0 vote had already been taken by the partners, including Aaron Luck and Jim Bodin, without me present. The four voted to close down the entire office for the next two days. That was on Thursday and Friday, May 28–29, 2020. That was if the Coronavirus would somehow dangle in the office air for an entire week. Hoping to elicit better cooperation from me through reverse psychology, Kenneth and Joe compared me to "Donald Trump wanting to keep everything open." They believed this slight would motivate me, as a Biden delegate to the Democratic National Convention, to join them in closing.

"No dice," I quickly replied: "I don't buy it." So, what if I sided with Trump, I said. I agreed with him on some things. That was especially about keeping the economy open. Even though the other four had outvoted me, I reminded Kenneth and Joe that I alone owned the building. I had anticipated this day coming, I told them "Come hell or high water," I'd be there the next two days at our 516 S. Perry Street office, along with Leslie, to handle business and clients, even if no one else were there.

Fortunately, my All-Star office manager, Amy Strickland, bless her heart, was very loyal. Less fearful, she decided that if I were coming in, she too would come in to help me and relieve my wife, Leslie. I was exceedingly grateful to Amy, and although aggravated by the unnecessary fears of the other partners, I tried to be understanding. Partner Joe Guillot nonetheless did come in briefly that Thursday to finalize a settlement with a client. No one else dared set foot into our supposedly dangerous office building. I knew better . . . there was nothing dangerous. I had absolutely no fear. And this was during the height of the hysteria.

Good that I did come in. At 9:30 that Thursday morning, May 28, 2020, David Sawyer called me from his Birmingham home office, saying we had a pre-trial conference that morning in federal court in Montgomery in a case involving Montgomery firefighter client Frank Bolling. David had previously understood it would be by Zoom from his home but had just discovered otherwise. He asked me to cover for him in Montgomery's federal court that morning. I gladly agreed.

I was elated to do so, for two reasons. First, it proved how wrong my partners were in trying to close the office down. More importantly, I could hardly wait to get back into court "to see, smell, and breathe the courtroom . . . and keep my tools sharp." So, I quickly passed through security on the ground floor of the federal courthouse. Young, newly appointed Judge Andrew Brasher, on the fourth floor, could not have been nicer. He, too, was ready to try the case. All cylinders were on go for a June 2020 federal jury trial, as Brasher gave additional pre-trial deadlines.

This was especially significant because presiding Montgomery County Circuit Judge Johnny Hardwick personally informed me that very same morning of May 28 that due to Coronavirus the Montgomery County Courthouse would be closed until mid-September 2020. How unnecessary, I thought. Little did I realize how much longer jury trials would actually be forbidden . . . all the way to May 2021 at the Dallas County Circuit Court in Selma. The more Caucasian counties of Elmore, Autauga, Chilton, and Lee were open as early as June 2020, and remained so throughout the pandemic. Most of the majority-Black counties were more cautious and closed.

Federal Judge Brasher, though new to the bench, was and is smart and conscientious. He was known for being more conservative on plaintiff employment cases. David and I were taking on the City of Montgomery, known for rarely settling cases. Yet the judge had ruled in our favor on two of three counts in the Kenneth Bolling case, denying the defense's summary judgment motion. Judge Brasher was as eager as we were to try the case and doled out various pre-trial deadlines to attorneys in June 2020. Unfortunately, two weeks later courthouse security overruled him, amidst growing Covid concerns, and caused the trial to be postponed for another 15 months until September 2021, and then six months more to February 2022, then again to May 2022.

Back to mid-2020.

The next week, June 1–5, 2020, I was in Elmore County District Court, twice before Judge Glenn Goggins, once on a civil case, and the other on a criminal case. I also had a virtual trial before District Judge Tiffany McCord of the Montgomery County District Court. The following week (June 8–11), I was at the Chilton County Courthouse in Clanton to defend my paralegal's husband, Brad Jackson. Then back to the Elmore County Circuit Court before Judge Reynolds to help defend client Clayton Thomason.

On June 3, 2020, I participated in an Unemployment Compensation final appeal hearing for client Elizabeth Smith before the State Labor Department's Appellate Hearing Board. This hearing was the first since the mid-March 2020 Corona restrictions set in that I was actually required to wear a mask as a condition to entering the building. Everyone in the hearing room was wearing masks. All of us struggled with muffled speaking, challenged breathing, and a degree of coughing.

By the end of that week, Friday, June 12, 2020, Leslie and I took our first out-of-state travel break in three months. We popped up first to Lake Martin to catch our son David, his pregnant wife Melinda, and our daughter Grace and her two young daughters, Nanette and Emmanuelle. We then headed southeastward to St. Simons Island, Georgia, on the Atlantic Coast. Very few were masked at St. Simons, not surprisingly.

As previously stated, I learned during the pandemic what I never knew before. To the surprise of many, my blood type, "O-negative," was a great buffer against not only Corona but other viruses as well. I learned this from multiple reliable sources, first from Terry Strickland (office manager Amy's husband), also O-negative, who cited a CNN News report that the 6 percent of American citizens with O-negative had a good protection against the Corona bug. A copy of the report I obtained verified the same. Certain of my family members were unconvinced, believing I was naive.

On the flip side, an O-negative person can give blood to any other blood types. Yet, we O-negatives can only receive blood from other O-negatives, that same small 6 percent of the population. That part is no advantage, but it motivated me to give blood, which I did six times in both 2020 and 2021, and at continuing two-month intervals in 2022.

In May 2020, I learned more. The next was client Tony Stephens, ex-fire chief of the City of Selma, long involved in paramedic work. Chief Stephens said, "Oh, you have O-negative . . . lucky you, you must never have the flu." My response was "virtually never," except for one brief time in early 2001 when I went out to Baptist South Hospital to spend the night with my son David. Coming out of his room the next day, in January 2001, a whiff of a bad SARS-type flu from another patient hit me. I felt terrible that first day, but only for a few hours, and then quickly it all disappeared, completely shaken off. Amazing, I thought at the time. In hindsight, I realized it was the immunity strength of my blood type. Yet, I had never heard of anything like this in the 73 years of my life before Corona.

The next to inform me was Belinda Humphrey of Auburn, a 30-year hospital administrator at the East Alabama Medical Center in Opelika. She said, "Oh, you have O-negative; you must never be sick." And I said, "almost never," recounting that the only episode of real illness in the last 50 years, besides a rare cold or athletic injury, was a psychological illness experienced in 2006. That was a depression induced by an excessive thyroid medication wrongfully prescribed by an osteopath who was outside her field.

Further confirming this O-negative immunity is that both my wife Leslie and paralegal Bridget Strength in January 2020 had extremely disabling two-week cases of the flu. In hindsight, we believed both had many characteristics of Corona. Yet as close as I was to each, one at the office, the other at home, I caught nothing from either.

Ample written documentation exists, I have since learned, confirming that the O blood type, whether positive or negative, but especially O-negative, is better than other blood types at resisting the Coronavirus. Out of gratitude, I continued my regular donation. I was also ecstatic to learn in December 2020 that three rare percolates in my own blood type (but not necessarily in other O-negatives) helped save the life of a local person desperately ill with sickle-cell anemia. What a Joy! I could hardly wait to help again. And thank you, Lord.

While I understand that many skeptics and cynics scoff at this suggestion, one-page written daily devotionals were a weapon much utilized by our law office against the pandemic. Comments were added about practicing safety protocol, but also practicing faithfulness, as we frequently cited 2 Chronicles 7:14, Ephesians 6:10–17, and James 1:2–3, among my favorite verses. Employees seemed to appreciate these messages. Many told me so.

As of July 31, 2021, sixteen months after we began protocol and devotionals, most of the 16 people from our office (eight attorneys and eight staff members), had been COVID-free. However, in November and December 2020, several did contract the virus. Yet all had light cases. Likewise, my immediate and extended personal families had no cases. Thank you, Lord!

Having shared the fortunate experience of my office and family, I nonetheless detested, and was deeply disturbed by the high toll of lives taken, and injuries inflicted nationally, and worldwide, by the Coronavirus. This bully has notoriously killed many people, injured, and maimed others, and caused great financial ruin or depression to many. Unfortunately, a spike in suicides—including a 20 percent annual increase in the military, also resulted. I pray for all these people . . . pray that their new lives beyond the grave, beyond planet earth, will be much better, and that the survivors on earth will recover.

My extended family was also involved in the fight. I am proud of my brother Frank for developing a well-respected daily blog on the toll of the virus, state-wide and nationally. He had many subscribers and readers. I am also super proud of my three grown children Rachel, Grace, and David, their spouses, and our seven grandchildren, all of whom took special precautions while remaining faithful, during the pandemic. While I sometimes thought their precautions were excessive, I agree it is "better to err on the side of caution, than to err the other way."

One grandchild, Julia McPhillips, daughter of David and Melinda was born October 11, 2020, amidst the scarier earlier months. Meanwhile, during the two-year pandemic, our daughter Grace, at age 40 and a half, gave birth to her third child, her first son, and our seventh grand- on July 11, 2021. The young fellow's name was Lucien "Luca" Lunsford. He was eleven pounds two ounces and twenty-two inches, so his mom gave birth by her first C-section. Bravo, Grace!

While we lost no clients to the Corona bug, nonetheless one very dear to us, Mellie Dudley, 78, an age discrimination client of mine and Finney's, although remaining healthy herself, lost two daughters to COVID. They were Phyllis Floyd, at 54 an RN, and the other, Angela Lowry, at 58 an MD. They were her only children. Another client, Mary Robinson, lost her husband but recovered herself. Other clients caught the virus, but most had light cases, or recovered well. Thanks be to God! Finney and I continued to help Dudley combat the age discrimination case, though it became entangled in the arbitration albatross. Accordingly, given her tragedy, we gave her the entire settlement amount, taking no attorney's fee for ourselves.

Our country badly needs a fourth Great Awakening, or a spiritual revival akin to earlier Great Awakenings sweeping our country in the Revolutionary War era times of the 1700s and in the pioneer days of the 1800s or early 1900s. Indeed, our whole modern world badly needs this kind of change in a big way . . . ! While I realize that skeptics and cynics will scoff, I nonetheless know, as a student of history and theology, that such movements have accomplished much in earlier eras.

The Corona bully virus has truly been "the worst of bullies" . . . picking especially on people with underlying health issues and/or compromised immune systems, unable to fight it off.

From March 2020 through July 2021, I was frequently in and out of court in certain surrounding counties (Elmore, Autauga, Lee, Lowndes, and Chilton) where masks were early required, but after March 2021 not so much. Montgomery County on the other hand took much longer to open back up, except for Judge Brook Reid's open courtroom, rife with masks. On the contrary, throughout the pandemic, Leslie and I enjoyed a variety of restaurants and stores, still open or struggling to remain so.

One of my cases in June 2020 took me to a Lee County dump site where we gathered with 30 African Americans in close proximity. None of us caught anything. Ditto for a trial in Opelika Municipal Court in November 2020, another trial in the Auburn Municipal Court in December 2020, and another trial in the Bessemer District Court of Jefferson County in February 2021. In all this, I say, again, "Thanks be to God!" Meanwhile, many people we respected, although certainly not ourselves, were living in a cocoon or bubble, and surviving this way. Obviously, and making big news, were others we did not know, who died.

As alluded earlier, in the last two months of 2020 our law firm finally encountered a few bumps on the COVID radar screen. On my 74th birthday on November 13, 2020, law partner Joe Guillot tested positive. But he stayed home for 14 days of quarantine, received little medication or doctor's attention and no hospitalization, despite receiving radiation for a pre-existing skin cancer. Joe's faithfulness helped, I am sure, as did his O-positive blood. Boosted by much prayer, Joe shook it off quickly and quietly, soon testing negative.

Likewise, Amy Luck and Mary Bodin, wives of law partners Aaron and Jim, and both nurses, tested positive but had relatively light cases, and quickly recovered. Despite the close proximity, neither firm husband came down with it. And then long-time firm runner and firm chaplain Kaylon Jenkins tested positive. What a man of faith he is. He quarantined at home, felt okay most of the time, and returned to work in two weeks. Finally, receptionist-paralegal Crystal McQueen also caught it, struggled a bit, but recovered quickly. She has been an angel in helping me send out the firm's daily devotionals. Thank you, Crystal, and thank you, Cesaire McPherson, and Stephany Moore for also helping.

Compared to the constant bombardment of daily damage reported in the media, we know that the McPhillips Shinbaum firm's experience has been quite fortunate. We dodged the bullet daily. Most of us, me included, have had two vaccinations but we've had a few holdouts. We also regularly thank God for life itself, good health, peace, prosperity, and many other foundational blessings.

THIS HAS BEEN GRADUALLY supplemented, written contemporaneously to address the first two years of containment, from March 16, 2020, through March 16, 2022. With Joe Biden's election as president and his assuming office in January, vaccinations accelerated in 2021. I am now optimistic about the world's recovery from the bully pandemic. Our firm's Coronavirus containment (CVC) efforts, empowered by the Holy Spirit's power, and aggressive scientific protocol, including vaccinations, has been successful. I expect much more to be written in future years about this crazy era of mankind's history. Although more may be written on the scientific side, the spiritual side needs to be recognized and appreciated.

By the mid-March 2021 date, my dear wife Leslie had already had her two vaccinations, as had my brother Frank and wife Louise, daughters Rachel and husband Jay, and son David and wife Melinda. I got my first vaccination on April 1, 2021, and second on May 13, 2021. Although I felt a "yucky" fatigue, (with no headache or stomachaches) on the second day after the vaccination, I did fine by the third day after both shots. These vaccinations were necessary to attend my dear nephew Dixon McPhillips's wedding celebration in Los Angeles on July 2–4, 2021.

As stated in my family's annual 2020 Christmas card, I said this year ranks fully with, if not exceeding, the years 1865, 1918, 1929, 1941, 1968, and 2001 as the most significant in U.S. history. My hope and prayer were that 2020–2021 would be remembered as a period of transformation, healing, revival, and renewal. It has been so for me and many others.

As for the law firm, 2020 and 2021 turned out to be two of our best years ever of the 21st century. As for my faith, it has been strengthened by the knowledge that the same God who heals cancers can just as easily provide a shield during a pandemic virus and stop or heal anything else.

## The Fourth Wave

And just when we believed that the great vaccination surge of March and April 2021 was about to send the Corona Bully scurrying away, the infamous "Fourth Surge" started gaining momentum.

I tried two cases before juries, once in Tuscaloosa in May 2021 defending Jordan Thomas, the second in June 2021 in Montgomery defending Willie Burks. Masks were required during the "Voir Dire," that is, "picking of the jury," but after that, the court let us drop our masks if we were vaccinated.

In September 2021, I heard about a new surge of the Delta variant of COVID, apparently fueled by the large number of unvaccinated people, with Alabama infamously again leading the pack's statistics.

In our law office, the only casualty was a brief one, namely our dear 24-year employee Page McKee, who caught it from her kids, who caught it at school. But Page was out no more than two weeks and returned healed well and spirited. Although she briefly went to a hospital, she was soon out.

The only other issue, not really a controversy, was that five of our most important employees, all female, were opting not to have the vaccination. What was going on? That included office manager Amy Strickland, whose wisdom and discretion I have long respected. It also included paralegals Cesaire McPherson, Wendy Newman, Page McKee, and Dana Simon, all of whom I also respect. Three of them felt otherwise and got their shots, namely attorney Tanika Finney, paralegal Crystal McQueen, and attorney Andrea Hatchcock, newly hired in October 2021.

One Friday night, August 27, 2021, upon arriving at our Lake Martin "McP Retreat," I heard the TV news about the upcoming Hurricane Ida, bearing down on New Orleans and Baton Rouge. Having already checked on my Dixon cousins fleeing to Dallas, I called Dr. Fred Billings, a Princeton classmate and a dear friend of 57 years, a resident of Baton Rouge. I meant to invite Fred and his wife Susan up to Alabama, and away from the storm. Instead, before I could say much, I received a half-hour lecture from him about how, and why, I was so irresponsible not to require all my employees to get the vaccination, as a condition of their continued employment. I told Fred, "I can't make them do that," as they were all my valuable employees and I'd lose as much, if not more, than they would, if I wouldn't let them return unvaccinated. Fred, however, kept verbally batting me around in a droning, authoritarian voice, only occasionally interrupted by a deep chuckle.

Meanwhile, in September and October 2021 several big trials were looming, and on Labor Day weekend the SEC football season kicked off with its 100,000-seat stadiums filled with the unmasked and unvaccinated. Prophets of doom and gloom were everywhere making their dire predictions, calling it a "super spreader." It was not really.

Unfortunately, cultural battles persisted between those favoring vaccinations and those against, with the added sub-issue of whether governmental or business mandates were appropriate. Another battle percolated, and sometimes exploded, between those favoring wearing masks, and those against.

And again, I thought, "Where is God in all of this?" The answer is in 2 Chronicles 7:14. On Sundays Leslie and I listened regularly at our Lake Martin place to what the Rev. Jay Cooper and other spiritual leaders were saying, citing the Gospels and Epistles, while offering Holy Spirit-inspired answers. Meanwhile, we drove home regularly to Montgomery many late Sunday afternoons to enjoy praise and worship services on the front porch of our Old Cloverdale home. Again, the musicians were masked; but we were not. Yet we all belted out songs of hope and purpose in putting the virus in retreat, and re-establishing Jesus in the consciousness of our lives.

## The Fifth Wave

Just as we thought the Corona virus was largely receding, a fifth wave, originating in South Africa, sprang up overnight. It was called the "Omicron," wherever that word came from. It appeared to be quite contagious, but its symptoms and effects were much milder. Some equated it to the "common flu" but others in authority spoke in more ominous tones.

Our law firm, with signs about masks no longer present on the doors of entry, treated it casually. Our daily devotionals encouraged employees to practice both scientific protocol, carefulness, and faithfulness.

During this time, especially from late October to early December 2021, it was "boomtimes" financially for the firm. I had five substantial settlements, all from employment cases, swelling our firm's coffers. Indeed, I repeated that 2020–2021 turned out to be "two of our best years ever, thank you, Lord."

With Thanksgiving and Christmas vacation 2021 fast approaching, we visited first our daughter Grace and her family in Atlanta on Turkey Day, and then Rachel and her crowd in Huntsville for Christmas. No special precautions were taken, but son-in-law Corbett Lunsford in Atlanta "gently subjected" Leslie and me to some kind of Q-tip nasal test before allowing us to enter, maskless, into the rest of his house, to visit with our three Lunsford grands.

Two big jury trials were coming up for me in the New Year 2022, one a criminal defense case of Correctional Officer Devlon Williams for using excessive force against an inmate, starting January 4, 2022. The second, on January 24, 2022, involved a defamation defense of former U.S. Senate candidate Roy Moore, for simply denying what a female accuser, Leigh Corfman, had said about him (see Chapter 17).

By the end of 2021, the Justice Department in Washington convinced partner Joe Guillot and me to agree to a continuance of the Williams case, due to the highly contagious Omicron virus. On the other hand, on December 30, 2021, the lawyers in the Moore case had a three-hour zoom conference with Judge John Rochester. This case was still set in concrete to begin on time, January 24, subject to further check the week before. That is because, the Montgomery County Circuit Court continued all jury trials for the weeks of January 4 and 11, 2022, due to the new coronavirus surge.

## 2022

On January 3, 2022, I passed out to office employees the 478th daily CVC email devotional. Our firm has remained in the coronavirus battle and law practice for the long haul, continuing our combination of scientific precaution and faithfulness well into 2022. On Sunday January 16, 2022, amidst snow, ice, and 35 degrees outside, our monthly front porch praise and worship service of the past two years moved inside our house, in front of a roaring fire.

The praise and worship services continued on the last Sundays of the month during the year 2022. Meanwhile, the legal business was as busy as ever, and, disregarding any corona threat, Leslie and I were excitedly planning our first trip out of the United States in three years on April 16–30, in the Netherlands, with approximately thirteen classmates and wives from my Princeton Class of 1968. And then on to Denmark and Greenland in July, and Brazil in December.

But my first two jury trials of 2022 are worthy of COVID comment.

The first running from January 24–February 2, involved a successful defense of former Alabama's Supreme Court Chief Justice Roy Moore against a defamation lawsuit. Notable is that no jury trials at all were held in the Montgomery County Circuit Court for the preceding three weeks, due to renewed COVID fears. Since the Moore trial started on the fourth Monday, we began tentatively. All jurors, attorneys, assistants, and Judge Rochester wore masks, and sixteen jurors were selected with four as alternates, in case jurors contracted COVID.

The second jury trial, a criminal defense of correctional officer Devlon Williams, did not begin until May 9, but ended with a hung jury, always a victory for the defense. Masks were not required, but of the fifty juror prospects to choose from a panel, about half and half racially, the African Americans mostly wore masks, but none of the Caucasians did. What did that say?

Another interesting commentary is that in late April 2022, of the twenty-six returning Princeton classmates and spouses from a trip to the Netherlands, fifteen tested positive for COVID, but none felt badly. Leslie and I were two of the negatives . . . thanks be to God, because it could have interfered with the Williams trial starting that second weekend of May, soon after our return.

Our excitement in February and March 2022 was greatly tempered and wounded, in heart and soul, by the brutal Russian invasion of Ukraine. Comparative concerns about the coronavirus seemed to have evaporated.

On the weekend of June 11–12, 2022, our extended family met in

Huntsville for the renewed wedding vows of our son David and his wife Melinda, whose earlier planned ceremony of April 5, 2020, was scuttled by the first Corona outbreak. They had a beautiful event with well over 100 people coming in from all over the U.S.A. and Europe. As with two years and two months earlier, I served as the officiant, but this time also gave a homily, expanding upon similar words used by my father, the Rev. Julian L. McPhillips Sr., at the weddings of his first two grandchildren. The European contingent consisted of our daughter Rachel and her family. Unfortunately, our two grandsons in Germany, Jude and Sage, had to stay back home with their father due to Covid, while Rachel, upon arriving in America, had to quarantine, as she apparently caught Covid from her sons. Meanwhile, granddaughter Laurel, coming over with Rachel, attended the wedding and afterwards enjoyed a great week at Camp McDowell in the woods of northwest Alabama. At this late stage, June 2022, but with a lesser variant among vaccinated family members, Covid only took a bite out of us, causing minimal damage.

Likewise, from July 13–17, 2022, during our travels in Denmark and Greenland, we saw many people of all nationalities wearing masks, but the clear majority did not. Neither of us was touched by anything remotely Covid-like. In the airport, masks could be seen, but few were worn.

Even more amazingly, and light years away from the hysterical fears of March 2020, people in July–August 2022 were still getting Covid, but a much lighter variety. No big deal. It was like flu, but not a bad variety.

We humbly give God all the glory and honor for our good fortune, and pray that others who became sick, or went to Heaven, will rejoice in His provision and healing.

After all, I've heard it said and believe it that the greatest healing of all is when we shed our earthly body, like a caterpillar, and catapult into our Heavenly body. Or is it floating up?

# 5

# The Four Ladies of Integrity

Bullying comes in various sizes, shapes, and personalities. This I learned again from November 2017 to April 2018 when visited by four ladies of great integrity, each one bullied by ACES (the Alabama Cooperative Extension Service), long headquartered on the Auburn University campus. Their common denominators were their genders and older ages. All were Caucasian, thus race was not an issue, but sex and age were.

The ladies came from different corners of Alabama. Margaret Odom, 66, was from Chatham, of remote and rural Washington County, just north of Mobile. Her attorney husband, Harold Odum, was a seventh-generation descendant from the pioneer inhabitants of St. Stephens, the early territorial capital of Alabama before it became a state in 1819. Margaret was the first of the four to see me, on November 5, 2017.

The second, Sally Hooker, at 73 the oldest, came from Selma to see me on February 15, 2018. She had reached 75 when the case was resolved.

Thirteen days later, the third, Wanda Carpenter, 66, came up from the Wiregrass city of Dothan in southeast Alabama, near Florida and Georgia.

The fourth, Melanie Allen, came from Rogersville in northwest Alabama, near Mississippi and Tennessee. The youngest of the four, she was 57.

All four were Regional Extension Agents ("REAs") at ACES. All, once happy, had become quite dismayed by the disrespectful, cold, and hostile way they were being treated by four older white men running ACES, (aka "the Extension Services") namely Drs. Paul Brown, Kyle Kostelecky, and Gary Lemme, and Stanley Windham.

The women had similar stories. All were deeply distressed, so we filed charges of sex and age discrimination with the Equal Employment Opportunity Commission in Birmingham. My associate attorney Chase Estes and I shared their indignation and dismay. We were highly motivated to help them take on the bullies.

Each client described a "good ol' boy" network, top-heavy with senior white men in leadership positions. The four plaintiffs had all been relegated to what were unofficially considered "female jobs." They were paid less than younger men doing similar work.

At the fateful November 2017 meeting ACES announced, they were transitioning these REAs into new "human science" positions during the next two years. Each would be housed on the Auburn University campus by December 31, 2019. This set off shockwaves. It signaled to each lady the "coming of their terminations," more sterilely described as "job eliminations."

If the new transition had been implemented, Odom would have had to commute more than four hours each way to Auburn University, or relocate from her Chatham dwelling (where her husband was in law practice, making a family move impossible). Or she could enter an early retirement. Allen had an equally distant trip from her northwest corner of Alabama. Hooker would have to commute from Selma to Auburn, a four-hour round trip. Carpenter's commute from Dothan to Auburn would be a six-hour round trip. For all four, this was a big time "no go."

The transition and moves were the joint brainchild of the four older white men, sparked by Kostelecky, a fairly recent arrival from Iowa, which is near where Lemme and Brown also originated.

Such a move would also have caused upheaval for many other REAs from around Alabama. They were all unhappy but more cautious about the cost of time and money in challenging ACES in court. Thus the others got a free ride from the sacrificial efforts of the four ladies who paid significant fees for legal representation.

The biggest bully in the group was Kostelecky. He was described in the combined complaints of plaintiffs Allen, Hooker, and Carpenter, which were consolidated with Odom's earlier suit. The cold, hostile working environment was outlined by the four ladies in a court-filed complaint (paragraphs 43–38) as follows:

Dr. Kostelecky has often bragged that, since he began working with ACES, he has "fired nine employees." Although the discharged employees might not have been directly supervised by Dr. Kostelecky. He nonetheless but routinely used this information to intimidate and threaten the plaintiffs, and other older female FCS Agents. (Para. 43).

Condescendingly, during a team meeting, Dr. Kostelecky read *The Wretched Stone*, a children's book, to FCS REAs as if they were children. The book concerned sailors finding a curious stone, which slowly turns them into apes. When a storm breaks the stone, the sailors "return to normal." The plaintiffs and other REAs questioned why Dr. Kostelecky chose to read them a children's book reflecting, as it did, Dr. Kostelecky's growing distaste for the REAs. This contributed to a pervasive cold and hostile work environment toward the plaintiffs. (Para. 44).

In another meeting, Dr. Kostelecky told the plaintiffs and other REAs to turn their phones off and put them on a table in front, where he could see them. Dr. Kostelecky proceeded to lecture the plaintiffs and other REAs on "theory." He afterwards showed PowerPoint slides containing 12 pictures. One was of a chocolate chip cookie; another was of an oatmeal raisin cookie. Dr. Kostelecky stated that he "didn't like raisin cookies. He liked chocolate chip cookies. . . ." Therefore, if he "ate an oatmeal raisin cookie, thinking it was a chocolate chip cookie, he would spit it out." Dr. Kostelecky used the metaphor of a pigeon and a sparrow, comparing the REAs, mostly females, to pigeons, or the lowest of the low. Dr. Kostelecky was using these metaphors during the meeting to show his distaste for the plaintiffs and other REAs. (Para. 45).

Further, Dr. Kostelecky called the REAs "bullies" and said that they "needed therapy." This was completely out of line and untrue. Dr. Kostelecky also compared the REAs to mental patients. He even demonstrated their attempts to diminish their intelligence. (Para. 46).

In another meeting, Dr. Kostelecky stated that REAs do not have the "intellectual capacity" to perform certain duties expected. The plaintiffs were appalled and insulted at Dr. Kostelecky's insinuation, that they lacked intelligence. This was the second time Dr. Kostelecky had insulted the intelligence of the REAs. One REA responded, "we are smart, too!" (Para. 47).

On another occasion, Dr. Kostelecky brought a box of Kleenex tissues to the Hale County office. When asked if he needed the tissues because of allergy season in the South, Dr. Kostelecky stated they were for the Regional Extension Agents when he conducted their performance reviews. (Para. 48).

Working in advance to counter our strongest claims before filing anticipated summary judgment motions, the Extension Service made several strategic moves. First, it rescinded the plan to move all REAs to Auburn. A secondary plan greatly increasing the workload of three clients was scuttled.

Otherwise, ACES ignored the claims of our ladies under the Equal Pay Act that they were being paid less than male ACES employees for the same work.

Then the 2020 Corona wave hit. As one month stretched into another, March into May, ACES's skilled attorney Dorman Walker and I were talking logistics about coordinating twelve depositions, a burden neither side wanted. We finally broached the possibility of mediation. Before doing so, Walker said our $250,000 demand per client was "way out of line and needed to come down."

Meanwhile, another important development developed for my plaintiffs with the retaining of Dr. Linnda Durre as an employment discrimination expert. Coming from Winter Park, Florida, near Orlando, she had an extensive resume of accomplishments, more on gender issues than in the age field. I knew from her work on another case that Durre, though 72, had the energy of a 27-year-old. We called her the "Energizer Bunny." With a great deal of hard work, Durre prepared an expert witness report, encompassing three revisions. Unfortunately, the modest compensation eventually awarded barely covered the three revisions.

Conference calls, with our clients calling in from remote areas of Alabama, were awkward. Some of the older ones on the calls—including me—could barely hear the others, especially when everyone started talking simultaneously.

Enormous credit, we agreed, went to the youngest member of our team of seven, Chase Estes, 32. Chase, due to covid, had been holed up for months in his home apartment. He was working remotely on our ACES discovery responses without the interruption of office distractions. The ladies were answering many questions. They were even responding to document requests from ACES.

Finally, exchanges of letters between Dorman and me, which were aided by Durre's expert witness report, got us to the mediation table in the chambers of U.S. Magistrate Judge Jerusha Adams, an African American female. She was only recently appointed. This was Judge Adams's first mediation, where she did an excellent job.

Each client deserved a significant settlement. This was naturally where ACES resisted. The all-day struggle ended about 7:30 p.m. with the case finally "resolved," as we all agreed to call it, with strict confidentiality provisions to its terms. The ladies were happy, although Chase, much to his credit, kept responding to the ladies' lingering concerns. He did so for two more months, hammering out final agreements with Dorman. At the end of July 2020, the cases were put to bed. My clients were largely happy. To quote Shakespeare, "All's well that ends well."

Or is it? Different interpretations about the amount of back pay could be credited for the Retirement System of Alabama (RSA) purposes because of a lingering and unresolved sore. We had two clients leading the charge. In the end, I crafted another motion leading to a Zoom hearing on September 9, 2020, before Judge Adams, the magistrate who had previously functioned as mediator. ACES and Dorman were fairly neutral on the issue. Unfortunately for us, RSA's general counsel <u>Leura</u> Canary argued in stringent opposition. Magistrate Adams ruled against us, holding that nothing could be added to the retirement nest egg my client had previously accumulated at RSA.

In the end, Margaret Odom, Sally Hooker, Wanda Carpenter, and Melanie Allen reflected enormous integrity and courage. In their lifetimes, each has done much to make Alabama a better state and help its citizens. I enormously admire their perseverance and fortitude in standing up to bullies. It was my honor, and Chase's, to represent them. Dorman Walker also represented Auburn well.

# Travel Is Good for the Spirit

In my previous books, I have enjoyed sharing traveling experiences, mostly at an international level. My wife Leslie was born in Brazil, but she was educated in Switzerland. She did not come to the USA until 1971. We met in 1973, following my wrestling in the Eastern AAU Championships. Our first trip abroad together was in 1974, as part of our honeymoon.

Leslie had traveled abroad before ever coming to the USA. I had been to France for a study period while I was in college. And when my sister studying in Mexico, I visited her there. I gained more travel experience when my father was the first U.S. Peace Corps director in India. He and my mom lived in Kolkata (formerly Calcutta) the capital of India's West Bengal state. (Geographically part of the Bengal region, East Bengal existed from 1947 until 1955 when it was renamed East Pakistan. Today, the area is an independent country, Bangladesh.)

While working in New York City at American Express Company, I took advantage of excellent discounts on travel that brought me to Hawaii, Tahiti, and New Zealand and Australia.

In 1975, my new bride Leslie and I enjoyed a second honeymoon starting in Egypt riding camels and seeing pyramids before going to Kenya and Tanzania to see the famous Ngorongoro Crater. From there we traveled to South Africa, visiting Angola briefly before arriving in Brazil to meet Leslie's childhood friends. That was when I received word from my dear mother that I had passed the Alabama Bar Exam.

We returned to the USA in May 1975, in time to pack up in New York City to move down to Alabama. Over the years, we took Caribbean cruises with the Alabama Trial Lawyers, and another cruise from New York City through Maine to Nova Scotia, where we saw remnants of the Titanic in a museum dedicated to that disaster.

As time passed, we found ourselves traveling all over the world. That included a total of five trips to Africa and five trips to South America in the Southern Hemisphere. We often have said our best trip was to Antarctica on a French ship. There we saw thousands of penguins, many whales, walruses, and other wildlife on the seventh continent of the world.

In 1990, we went Israel for three weeks and returned in 1995. Faith in Christ undergirds our attitude, and this has been passed on to our children, who also love to travel.

Leslie and I both enjoy our family life in Alabama. That has included many weekend trips to the Gulf Coast from 1983 up to 2023 when we had a condominium at the Gulf Shores Plantation Resort. We also secured a cottage at Lake Martin in 1985 and have enjoyed it with largely weekend trips from then to the present.

In our older ages, at 75 (Leslie) and 76 (me), we have slowed down, but only a small bit. In April 2022, we began two interesting trips to Europe. The first was to the Netherlands, with a group of 13 classmates and 12 spouses. We were a merry band traveling around Holland seeing tulips, windmills, and wooden shoes as well as the International Court of Justice and The Hague. The second trip three months later was to Denmark in Greenland. At the time this account was written in 2023, we were planning a trip to Germany to see our oldest daughter Rachel, her husband Jay, and their three precious children Laurel, Jude, and Sage.

In the pandemic years of 2020–2021, we especially stayed closer to home. We enjoyed the proximity of the Southern states, with the exception of a California trip for a nephew's wedding in July 2021. These U.S. travels are described first. We returned to some international travel in 2022, and those accounts conclude this chapter.

## MISSISSIPPI MEDDLING, MARCH 2020

Traveling well does not mean traveling far. Nonetheless, two and a half months of virtually unabated law practice, along with church, museum, and family responsibilities, created a big need for a break. All work and no play is no fun and makes Julian a dull boy. He is to be avoided at all costs. Pacing oneself makes one sharper and more productive.

Leslie and I chose our neighboring state of Mississippi to catch our breath and enjoy the scenery. We began by popping northwestward to Tuscaloosa on Monday, March 9, 2020, to enjoy the Writer's Hall of Fame banquet. Fitzgerald aficionados filled two tables of ten. We cheered for Zelda, as she was posthumously awarded entry into this newly famous Literary Hall of Fame. Humor, wit, and literary inspiration sparked the evening. The youngest of the seven winners was Michael Knight Jr., a second cousin once removed, from my ancestral homeland of Mobile. I had never met him before, although I knew his parents, Barbara and Michael Knight Sr. Facially, however, there was a strong McPhillips imprint.

Early the next morning, we bounced ninety miles over to Starkville, Mississippi, to see a new friend, Sarah McCollough. She manages the Ulysses Grant Museum at Mississippi State University. We especially enjoyed the Museum's Abraham Lincoln exhibit. We also saw the John Grisham Extension Hall, subsidized by MSU's homegrown but now famous author.

Tuesday, we were on the road again, weaving 45 miles southwest to French Camp, with its historic French Camp Academy co-founded in the 1880s by my great-grandparents James and Ellen Sanderson. They were pioneer educators whose legacy and 40 years of leadership is much celebrated there. We knew that our son David would have enjoyed teaching there, given the school's emphasis on training students with diverse needs. Development director Lance Ragsdale drove us around the campus, pointing out new buildings springing up between time-battered fixtures.

By mid-afternoon, we headed north along the pioneering Natchez Trace, enjoying Indian mounds, stagecoach trails, and a long-untouched forest interior. We arrived in Tupelo, with its proud history of native son Elvis Presley, whose childhood home and related memorabilia were quite interesting. Remembering his musical presence of the 1950s and '60s flashed us back to nostalgia land.

After a long day of traveling, we arrived 50 miles later in Oxford, the home of the University of Mississippi and its Ole Miss Rebels. Leslie and I checked into the "Inn at Ole Miss" on campus. We then backtracked into the town square, ending up feasting at a Cajun restaurant. The next morning, we toured the Ole Miss campus. We thoroughly enjoyed Rowan

Oak, the antebellum house where author William Faulkner lived from the 1920s into the 1960s. Local host Bill Griffith gave us a splendid tour. Especially noticeable was a forest of aging cedar trees, planted 150–180 years ago to ward off yellow fever. A mile-long hike through the woods from Rowan Oak to the University of Mississippi's Museum of History topped off the morning.

By early afternoon, amid a driving rain, we hit the road for Jackson, the state capital and the home of a spectacular Mississippi Civil Rights Museum. We relished this and the adjacent Mississippi Museum of History. We just barely caught this treasure before it was shuttered. The next day, Thursday, March 12, we learned that all public museums in Mississippi were being shut down by the Coronavirus tsunami. We received concerning telephone calls from my office manager back home about the looming public health crisis.

That Wednesday evening we arrived in Vicksburg and checked in at the 1830s Anchuca Historic Mansion & Inn. The next morning Jefferson Davis's great-great-grandson, Bertram Hayes-Davis, and his wife Carol, entertained us with an intriguing tour of Vicksburg. After a spirited lunch with the Davises, we popped over to the Vicksburg National Park and Cemetery to see a large and well-preserved battleground, the site of a three-month epic struggle led by Union generals Grant and Sherman against Confederate forces under General Pemberton, who was outnumbered 10–1 and lost.

Intriguing signs and markers on the Vicksburg waterfront depicted Vicksburg's extraordinary history. One commemorated the event four days after the initial shot fired on Fort Sumter in 1861. At that moment in history, 39 Union vessels were on their way to Vicksburg and were fired upon by the CSS *Arkansas*, widening the war front. Another marker records that in 1865, just after the war was over, a local riverboat built for 376 passengers but packed with 1,800 Union prisoners returning home, along with 200 civilians, exploded just before reaching Memphis, killing at least 1,800.

Our GPS led us out of Vicksburg to Natchez, just a short trip down the road into the southwest corner of the state. This city was founded in

1716 by the Spanish on a broad swath east of the Mississippi River. This colonial capital once bustled with dynamism and pioneer influence. As we motored in, we stopped first at Melrose, a majestic plantation house with large Doric columns, topped by a "widow's walk" on the roof (although the river was miles away). A magnificent stand of magnolias captured our attention. This was eight to nine magnolias grown together over several hundred years, giving the impression of one gigantic tree.

We enjoyed several other magnificent antebellum mansions and early 1800s cottages en route to the Grand Hotel in Natchez. The fourth floor gave us a spectacular view of the Mississippi River which seemed just outside our window. A railed sidewalk lining the cliff overlooking the river was picturesquely laden with historic markers. This was perfect for a jog before dinner. That night we thoroughly enjoyed supper at a local waterfront restaurant.

A good night's sleep and tasty breakfast powered us onward Friday, March 13, to explore the awesome Rosalie and Longwood mansions. The latter, standing six to eight stories high, is a miniature Taj Mahal. Only its first two floors were finished before the Civil War began, and nothing was completed in the years since. En route we passed through Centreville, Mississippi, the ancestral home of my grandfather Frank Dixon, my mother's father. We then finished with a five-hour dash to Gulf Shores, including a ferry ride from Dauphin Island to Fort Morgan.

At Gulf Shores Plantation, we rested and enjoyed a wonderful visit March 13–15 with Leslie's youngest brother, Keith Burton. We were sharing an eighth-floor condo, with a great vista of the beach. By mid-Sunday morning, we were zipping up I-65 back to Montgomery. We were arriving at the beginning of the modern-day historic Coronavirus era. That Sunday evening, with churches shuttered, we enjoyed a wonderful, Holy Spirit-filled worship service bellowing out praise and songs on the front porch of our own historic Old Cloverdale home, where Helen Keller and her sister enjoyed rocking chair visits for 30 years. The music was food for our hungry souls. Thirteen of us gathered at the first Corona era service of many to come. Participants included three races: African American, Chinese, and Caucasian. All were calling upon God to intervene in the looming crisis.

## Georgia on My Mind, June 2020

As Mississippi is an intriguing state to visit to the west, Georgia takes similar honors on the east. Its capital, Atlanta, is the capital of the South, although we call it "New York South." Our daughter Grace McPhillips Lunsford learned the acting trade in Chicago for 12 years. She returned homeward three years ago with her husband Corbett. Grace was the first daughter closer to her family. She discovered that Atlanta was a good place to live, with more acting opportunities than in the Windy City to the north. Her nickname and her husband's remained "Grace in Space" and "Corbett in Orbit."

The two orbiters built an eco-friendly model home on nearly three acres in the College Park neighborhood of southwest Atlanta, only 10 minutes from the airport. Thus, Georgia placed a solid grip on our youngest daughter, fueling her multi-dimensional talents. Grace has given birth to two beautiful baby daughters, Nanette in 2016 and Emmanuelle in 2018.

During my lifetime I've been to Atlanta many times, beginning with early childhood trips. I hitchhiked in 1964 from Sewanee, Tennessee, to Atlanta, where I won third place in the Southern Wrestling Championships. I was first arguing cases before the U.S. Court of Appeals in Atlanta in the 1980s–'90s. Secondly, it was a near-death experience in the Peachtree Hotel's underground garage in 1993. Thirdly, it was attending the Olympic Games in 1996.

I've always known the obvious, that the rest of Georgia is unlike Atlanta but much more like Alabama. Savannah resembles Mobile. Both states enjoy mountainous terrain in the northern sectors. Both have a love of sports, have won national championships, and have coastal waters.

During June 12–15 of Covid 2020, we drove to the Golden Isles of St. Simons Island, Sea Island, and Jekyll Island. They have intriguing histories and captivating beauty. That combination sucked us out of the Corona syndrome. We finished with a five and a half hour drive back to Montgomery.

Leslie and I popped up to Lake Martin that Thursday night to enjoy our children Grace, David, and Melinda. We also saw our two grands. That next morning, we hopped onto Highway 280 toward the Phenix

City-Columbus area. We then wove our way down to Albany, on to Tifton, and finally to St. Simon's Island, which I had never before seen.

### St. Simons Island

This island locale has a special place in my family's history. In 1942, Mom and Dad, according to their autobiography, enjoyed early marriage there while Dad was training for the U.S. Navy. They actually stayed at the Cloister, an old hotel dominating the smallish "Sea Island." That was where they romantically romped on the beach. My older sister Sandy was born in October that year. She was likely conceived there.

I had long wanted to see this mysterious and intriguing place my parents enjoyed so long ago. Leslie and I arrived at about 4 p.m. on Friday, May 13. We checked in at the Beach Club on Ocean Boulevard. The front overlooks the Atlantic Ocean. A walk on the beach followed by a swim in the pool energized a good start. Later we drove downtown and noticed a few people wearing masks. All were enjoying the subtropical, historic scenery. After a good seafood dinner, we soon fell asleep.

The next morning, we drove off to see the remnants of colonial Fort Frederica, which included a restored village, only a few miles from the touristy town of St. Simons. We delighted in the history of General George Oglethorpe and his colony of soldiers, bakers, and candlestick makers. That group included David McGowin of Scotland, a sixth great-grandfather, from whom my grandmother, Lillybelle McGowin McPhillips, and my father, Julian L. McPhillips Sr., are descended. That heritage now includes me, my siblings, children, and seven grands.

Also fascinating was the history of the early Anglican evangelists John and Charles Wesley, brothers credited with starting Methodism in America and in England. Another great itinerant evangelist, George Whitfield, friend of the Wesleys, also spent time there. Leslie and I ambled around the grounds and cemetery of historic Christ Church, dating from the early 1700s. That church is one of seven that founded the Protestant Episcopal Church of America.

Our final evening included dinner at a Mexican restaurant. We walked around the downtown area, taking in the sights and sounds, etc. Again, only a few tourists were wearing masks. That included us, despite the virus hysteria soaring elsewhere.

That next morning, Sunday, May 15, we located the historic St. Simons lighthouse and other surrounding historical sites. We shoved off about 11 a.m., cutting across rural parts of Georgia in a six-hour jaunt back to Montgomery.

### LaGrange

Who would think that the moderately-sized town of LaGrange, not far across the Alabama line on Interstate 85, would have so many interesting things worth seeing? It does, however, and on Saturday, February 14, 2021, Valentine's Day, Leslie and I drove over from Montgomery to take it in.

We had long heard about the Biblical History Center founded and developed by Dr. Jim Fleming, a renowned archeologist and theologian. We first met Jim in Montgomery about 1988 and paid for Mom and Dad to take a two-week trip to Israel to travel with him and a local Methodist group that year. We ourselves waited until two years later to visit Israel and see Jim's famous Tantur Village, halfway between Jerusalem and Bethlehem. Our 2021 visit to LaGrange brought us to a facsimile Israeli village during the time of Christ. This treat also included a delicious Passover dinner.

Later we drove into LaGrange and first enjoyed the picturesque town fountain with a statue of Marquis de Lafayette in the town center (his estate in France was named LaGrange). We also visited Jim's business partner, Hananiah Pinto, and his Biblical resources store. Last but not least, we soaked in the famous "Hills on Dales Estate," famous for its antebellum gardens and mansion built by Fuller Calloway. At this early date, only the camellias were in bloom. The tour of this 13,000-square foot home was designed to flow gracefully into its charming garden. By late afternoon, we drove back to our Lake Martin home in Alabama. We also enjoyed Valentine's Day while celebrating Leslie's 73rd birthday the next day.

Numerous return trips were made to Atlanta during 2020–2022 to see daughter Grace's growing family (including son Luca born on July 11,

2021); we also launched trips to Europe in 2022.

## Sweet Home Alabama, August 2020

To enjoy the Southeastern United States, Alabama should be at the top of your list. I entered life there in Birmingham on November 13, 1946, and grew up in Cullman for my first 13 years. During that time, we also summered in Guntersville and enjoyed extended family visits in Mobile. Leslie and I have lived in Montgomery for the last 47 years. Despite its many problems this magnificent state has been "Sweet Home, Alabama" for people of different philosophies, sizes, and colors. Also known as the "Heart of Dixie," it has much to see and experience.

I've fought many civil rights battles, both civil and criminal, for fellow Alabamians for whom this state has been much less than "sweet." Deeply regretted are the various misfortunes and injustices many have suffered. Leslie and I have endured three miscarriages, the suicide death of my brother David, and one state-wide election stolen and another sabotaged.

I honor and thank God for creating, redeeming, and sustaining me, and wouldn't be here without Him. My biggest human blessing had been an awesome wife and soulmate, Leslie. She was born and raised in Brazil but has been living in America since she was 19. We added three children, Rachel, Grace, and David, and now their spouses and our seven grandchildren. With roots deep in Alabama on both parental sides before it became a state in 1819, "Alabama is in my blood." That includes growing up in the 1950s and 1960s, in a wholesome country town and nearby lake, while attending Episcopal summer camps in northwestern Winston County and visiting Dad's hometown in Mobile. We also enjoyed family vacations in Gulf Shores. It also includes practicing law with clients from most of Alabama's 67 counties, while enjoying all of Alabama's major cities and most of its towns. The title of my last book was appropriately *Only in Alabama*. That doesn't count five years in Tennessee (1959–64), four years in New Jersey (1964–1968), and seven years in New York (1968–1975), gaining perspective and comparison, as well as traveling in all 50 states.

## Cullman

So why live or vacation in Alabama, the Heart of Dixie, especially in 2020–2021? First, COVID kept us closer to home. On August 8, 2020, Leslie and I set sail from Montgomery. We first stopped in Cullman, my boyhood home. A floodtide of memories included the school, church, and neighborhood. I grew up in the King Pharr Company 60–70 years ago and see that it is largely the same, although Dad's vegetable canning business is long gone. We also visited my first cousin John McPhillips, five years younger, and his wife Linda, and lunched with them at Cullman's renowned All Steak Restaurant, now located across from Cullman's historic First Methodist Church (where I was truly inspired by my first Vacation Bible School experience at age two in 1948–49).

## Huntsville

We motored up to Huntsville, only an hour away, and checked into Madison Motel, before doubling back to see our beloved family in Mooresville, just off I-65. It is always a joy to see our oldest daughter, Rachel, her husband, Jay, and our three grands, Laurel, Jude, and Sage. All were temporarily residing with Jay's parents during renovations at their Huntsville home. Five generations earlier, Julius Plucker the first was a mid-1800s German mathematician-scientist, prominent enough to be in the *Encyclopedia Brittanica*. He was the patriarch of Jay's family line dynasty. Our son-in-law Jay, or Julius Plucker V, is not pretentious despite his heritage, nor is his son Jude, my oldest grandson, 11 years old when this was written. His full name is Julius Plucker VI.

The next day Rachel and Jay showed us the exciting progress on their renovated home in the Jones Valley Drive neighborhood of southern Huntsville. Afterwards, we journeyed down country roads eastward towards DeKalb County, nestled in the foothills of northeastern Alabama's Appalachian Mountains, near the Georgia line. Fort Payne, the county seat, is the home of the world-famous band, Alabama, known for its dozens of number #1 country music hit songs.

### Bear Creek

Our ultimate destination was Bear Creek Cabins, three miles from Dogtown in the high-altitude, wooded terrain of Dekalb County, near the Little River Canyon National Preserve. On Sunday afternoon, we checked into a rustic log cabin with modern conveniences. There were five other cabins in the neighborhood camp, each with a good distance between one another in these backwoods, teeming with wildlife. While Leslie purchased groceries, I hiked along a sparse trail, using two long ropes to shinny down to a dried-up creek bed. That night we both relaxed our muscles in the cabin's hot tub on the side porch.

The next day, Monday, August 10, we returned to Fort Payne to view the encampment where thousands of Native Americans, mostly Cherokees, were forced to endure the infamous "Trail of Tears." We subsequently skedaddled over to DeSoto State Park with its myriad hiking trails, enjoying several. We visited DeSoto Falls, whose ancient waters were diminished by an extended drought. Archeological evidence confirms that in 1540 Spanish soldiers under Hernando DeSoto camped there.

That afternoon we explored Little River Canyon, skirting from one exciting overlook to another. The stifling heat and humidity cut short our hikes, but the views were spectacular. Leslie snapped some artistic photos at "Mushroom Rock," sticking up in the middle of the Perimeter Road, which circled the canyon.

### SEWANEE, TENNESSEE, AUGUST 2020

On our third day at Bear Creek, we crossed over the Alabama-Tennessee border with an hour-long journey up Interstate 59, through a sliver of Georgia. We then ambled southwestward near Chattanooga before popping up Cumberland Mountain to the university town of Sewanee. My family lived there from 1959–1962, with Dad attending the Episcopal seminary, while I benefitted from attending Sewanee Military Academy. The spectacular scenery has changed little in the 56 years since my graduation from SMA in 1964. The best experiences of that era of my life remain nostalgically tucked away in my memory bank. However, other parts, like marching to church on Sundays, and reveille at 5:45 a.m. in freezing weather, were less exciting.

Given the COVID era, the incoming college students at Sewanee's secluded, rustic, Gothic "University of the South" were all wearing masks. I reveled in seeing my family's still-standing seminary home. However, the Military Academy's grounds were long ago converted into seminary student housing. The 100-foot-tall white cross at the end of Academy Road majestically spills out over the mountain's cliff edge, inspiring all. We also enjoyed great bluff sites along a picturesque trail circling the mountain's perimeter. My infamous "bear growl" remained intact. While hiking, I scared a few students with it, coming up behind them on a mountain trail. We all enjoyed some good laughs, students included.

At lunch, we met former law professor, theologian, and highly productive author LaGard Smith, at 75, one year older than me. We traded books. He gave me his *Meeting God in Quiet Places* and *Darwin's Secret Sex Problem* in return for my *Only in Alabama*. How enlightening were his writings, especially about encountering the Divine in the Cotswold countryside of England. I later sent LaGard my first two books, *The People's Lawyer* and *Civil Rights in My Bones*. A new friendship had emerged.

Our final day, Thursday, August 13, began with a backwoods front porch Zoom judicial conference with Judge Marvin Wiggins of Greensboro, Alabama. Other attorneys and parties called in from Montgomery, Birmingham, and Selma. We shoved off late that morning, scooting down Lookout Mountain to Weiss Lake in Cherokee County. There we enjoyed a picnic lunch at the Civil War era "Cornwall Furnace," built in 1861–62 to manufacture war metal materials for Confederate troops.

From there, an easy few miles delivered us back into northwestern Georgia, as we journeyed south to Atlanta. We helped our daughter Grace and husband Corbett celebrate their 16th anniversary at their newly developing homestead in College Park. Thrilled we were every time we saw those two beautiful, energetic, wide-eyed little granddaughters, Nanette, then four, and Emmanuelle, then two. By Saturday morning, August 15, 2020, we returned to Montgomery, our week-long getaway ending much too soon.

## ALABAMA AGAIN, 2020-21

During most of the pandemic era of March 2020–March 2021, Leslie and I spent our weekends at Lake Martin, Alabama's biggest, oldest, and cleanest lake, only 45 minutes north of our Montgomery home. "The McP Retreat" gives us peace and quiet, and an enjoyment of nature, water, and one another. We've had this early retirement cottage since 1985. I greatly enjoy "swimming across the slough" nine months of the year, sometimes after running on adjacent country roads, or traipsing through the woods on hikes with Leslie. I also relish the opportunity to read and write. Some is legal work, but much has been devoted to this book, painting images with words. And of course, we always enjoy the grands and our grown children.

### Dauphin Island

Our next week-long Alabama journey was March 13–20, 2021, when we scooted down the Interstate to Dauphin Island. Originally planned had been a week-long jury trial in Montgomery on behalf of my client Mike Keller. It was then postponed to June, due to continuing Corona safety concerns for juries (see Chapter 8).

My childhood stories in Cullman in the late 1940s included Dad telling my siblings and me about pirates burying treasure on Dauphin Island, which is only a sandbar of an island southwest of Mobile. In more recent times, our growing family enjoyed taking ferries from Fort Morgan (where great-great grandfather James McPhillips Sr. was stationed during the Civil War) over to Dauphin Island.

The week of March 13–20, 2021, while headquartered at a Dauphin Island beach condo, we enjoyed biking, running on the beach, and swimming in the pool. We also frolicked in Bellingrath Gardens in nearby Theodore. The azaleas were just beginning to bloom, but the camellias were not as diverse as in our own Montgomery garden.

Tuesday was an interesting journey into Mobile. We started with a good visit with attorney-cousin Rosie McPhillips on Conception Street and enjoyed the Basilica of Immaculate Conception, established in 1703. This cathedral is where my great-great-grandparents James and Rose

McPhillips met in 1865. The cathedral's name was apt, since they went on to have 10 children. An afternoon journey to Ashland Place, Dad's childhood neighborhood, was fun, as was dinner that night with several McGowin cousins at the Blue Gill Restaurant on the causeway.

We braced the next day for a thunderous storm but didn't realize until Friday (3/19/21) how much cold weather it ushered in on the day we met my McPhillips cousins Julie and David Bagwell for a Ben Raines-guided tour of the Mobile-Tensaw Delta. We thoroughly enjoyed the wild scenery but the 48 degrees at 10 am, amidst a 20–30 mph boat wind, was inadequately shielded by our not-so-warm clothing. Ouch. In fact, it was painfully chilly.

Notwithstanding the uncomfortable finish, the week was restful. This was a special time for Leslie and me to get away together from the law office, breathe and pace ourselves.

### Tuscaloosa

The name apparently came from an ancient Choctaw Indian chief named Tuscaloosa. In the five hundred years since then, this early American fish camp evolved into the second capital of Alabama, the football capital of the United States, and the home of a very good university.

Growing up as a child in the 1950s in Cullman, I heard the name of Tuscaloosa, only an hour and 15 minutes southwest, frequently mentioned in our home. My older sister Sandy was planning her first year of college at the University of Alabama. This followed in the footsteps of our father, Julian L. McPhillips Sr. (Julian II), and Grandfather Julian B. McPhillips. (Julian I). This granddad, in 1915 just before WWI, was on the University of Alabama football team when the sport was played like rugby. He also won the school's gold elocution medal in 1915. We remain quite proud of "Poppy," who made it to 1978. He also helped me in my campaign for Alabama Attorney General that year.

On mother's side of the family, there has long been a strong Tuscaloosa connection, although she barely knew it, and so we didn't until later in our adult years. Her great-grandfather, the Rev. Dr. David Davidson Sanderson, was a co-founder in 1871 of what was then called the "Tuscaloosa

College for Black Preachers." The school's name was changed in 1895 to Stillman College, following the death of Sanderson's co-founder and closest friend, the Rev. Dr. Charles Alan Stillman of Tuscaloosa who outlived my great-great-granddad by four years.

Perhaps subconsciously influencing his descendants, including my mother, me, and my siblings is that Sanderson's church in Eutaw, south of Tuscaloosa, was half white and half black before, during, and after the Civil War.

I had only once previously had a jury trial in Tuscaloosa. That was a criminal case in state circuit court in 2010. Yet another jury trial, this one federal, brought me back to Tuscaloosa in 2021. This time my dear wife Leslie not only accompanied me but also assisted me in court. That was because law partner Joe Guillot withdrew at the last moment, following the mid-April death of his wife Maria. From May 3–7, 2021, Leslie and I camped out at the Embassy Suites Hotel in downtown Tuscaloosa. I worked hard, trying a case in federal court for five straight days, defending a 21-year-old correctional officer named Jordan Thomas.

During the evenings, in the vicinity of University Boulevard and Greensborough Avenue, we briefly enjoyed a few good restaurants, at our own personal expense, before returning to the hotel to prepare. Except for each day in court, and reviewing notes for the next day, we enjoyed this diverse experience away from my Montgomery law office. Several late afternoon jogs after court along the Black Warrior River refreshed me, as freighter barges slowly tugged by. When the trial was over, we also enjoyed antebellum homes in the vicinity and the University of Alabama complex. We were especially delighted in the newly arrived statue of a 45-foot-tall elephant, with tusks jutting upward, looking like a mastodon, and ballyhooed in the recent news. Roll Tide!

At one lunch break, we encountered university undergraduate honor students from New Jersey and North Carolina. They informed us that 62 percent of the student body now was from out-of-state, and many were on substantial scholarships. This was due in significant part to Alabama money Nick Saban and his football teams had generated.

The greatest adventure all week was in court. While the trial ended in a hung jury on all counts for my defendant Thomas and co-defendants Keith Finch and Kevin Blaylock, this was actually a huge victory in the legal world, since the U.S. Justice Department boasts a 97 percent criminal conviction rate. It helped to have as my co-counsel two renowned Birmingham criminal defense lawyers, Richard Jaffe and Emory Anthony, representing the other two defendants.

Not surprisingly, with the change of scenery and spirited courtroom drama, I returned to Montgomery recharged from the week-long trip to Tuscaloosa. Jordan was scheduled for a retrial in November 2021. Although my client had the best jury results of the three defendants in terms of not guilty votes, Jordan and I decided to part company for the retrial on November 1, 2021, due to different strategic ideas.

## ARKANSAS SOJOURN

Continuing our Southeastern sojourn, we visited the non-adjacent but neighboring Arkansas in the fall of 2020.

Known for its Razorback Hogs, the Ozark Mountains and the historic 1955 *Brown v. Board of Education* decision desegregating public schools. Arkansas was recently made famous as the home of Bill and Hillary Clinton. Their names now adorn Little Rock Airport.

There is the fabled Arkansas football team that left the Southwestern Conference in 1990 to join the Southeastern Conference, cementing its better regional bona fides.

Our reason for exploring this rustic state was much more personal. Our only son David, having moved to Subiaco, Arkansas, to teach and proctor at its renowned Catholic boarding school, was about to turn 30. His wife Melinda was imminently due to give birth. So we left Montgomery on October 2, 2020, drove eight hours, and stayed in Arkansas until October 8. Their firstborn child, a daughter Julia, did not emerge until three days later, on October 11. Our sixth grand! Back home in Alabama, we rejoiced in the baby's Zoom photos, as did Rachel, Grace, and their families. Our number was now 14.

What a beautiful country northwestern Arkansas is. Subiaco is both an abbey and an academy, founded in the 1870s by Benedictine monks, mostly coming from Germany. A majestic architectural gem, today it rises like a European castle on a hill. It can also be viewed from a country bend, down the road. The nearest big city, Fort Smith, is 47 miles due west, on the Oklahoma border.

Notwithstanding the Corona era, we enjoyed meals with David and Melinda on picnic tables just outside the Castle. We also celebrated David's birthday Sunday evening in a see-through plastic tent a few miles down the road. The nearest municipality, five miles in the opposite direction, is named "Paris." David and I played golf there one afternoon. The next day, Leslie and I enjoyed Mount Magazine State Park, at 2,700 feet the highest peak in Arkansas. The day following, after further time with David and Melinda, we visited the scenic Mount Nebo State Park. Both parks boast ample hiking trails, beautiful vistas, and natural scenery in the reddish colors of fall.

On our last full day in Arkansas, we journeyed west, then north, to Fayetteville, home of the University of Arkansas. That is pure Razor-back Country! We then popped up to Bentonville, home of the Waltons, founder of Walmart, and location of a world-class art museum named "Crystal Bridges." The afternoon was completed with an eastward journey to Eureka Springs to see the highly acclaimed Crown Thorn Chapel, an ingeniously crafted glass structure, held together by a few wooden beams.

The next day we left Subiaco Academy and motored back to Huntsville, stopping briefly in Conway, near Little Rock, to visit with Sewanee Military Academy classmate Jim Batchelor (we played football and wrestled together at SMA in 1961–64). Leslie and I arrived in Alabama later that day for an endearing 43rd birthday visit with daughter Rachel, her husband, and our three grands, Laurel, Jude, and Sage. The next afternoon, upon arriving home in Montgomery, we joined daughter Grace, husband Corbett, and their toddler daughters Nanette and Emmanuelle, who had popped over from Atlanta and greeted us at our Old Cloverdale home upon our return. No one was wearing masks in late October 2020, so COVID beware! We enjoyed the time together, and all of us stayed safe.

On October 11, 2020, precious little Julia Taylor McPhillips was born. Doubly honoring me, David and Melinda gave her my childhood nick-name "Jutsy."

Thanksgiving weekend, Wednesday–Sunday, November 25–29, 2020, came sneaking up on us quietly. All our children, Rachel, Grace, David and their spouses and children had long planned to meet in Subiaco to celebrate baby Julia's arrival. The newest family member baby Julia would be a scant month and a half old. At the last moment Grace and Rachel Zoomed in on us. The burgeoning Corona made it unwise to gather together. Our trip to Subiaco was thus canceled.

Instead, we looked forward to enjoying all three branches of our family for Christmas 2020 and New Year's 2021 holiday in Montgomery, Lake Martin, Huntsville, and Atlanta, masks or no masks. It was where we were all scattered.

Meanwhile, David continued to teach and proctor at Subiaco Academy until the end of the school year in May 2021. In the summer he moved to South Carolina and rented a home in Grier, about halfway between Greenville and Spartanburg. In the latter city he had a new teaching job at Oakbrook Academy, teaching science and religion to fifth and sixth graders.

Arkansas, we hope to see you again someday, if and when I retire more fully!

## CALIFORNIA, HERE WE COME

I have much respect for the most populous state in the country, with a territory stretching from Oregon to Mexico. Its diversity is renowned, its resources opulent, and its issues are on the cutting edge of what is happening in the rest of the country. California, we're coming again, drawn to you this time by a family wedding.

The first time I approached California was in 1967 when I was traveling with my siblings David and Betsy from the Orient on the way back from India. We stopped first in San Francisco, seeing the flower children in the Haight-Ashbury district. We stopped again in Los Angeles, enjoying Disneyland, before we all returned to northeastern colleges.

In 1990 we came again, following a trip to Alaska. Leslie and I ventured with our three kids into northern California, enjoying the redwoods and driving down to San Francisco.

It wasn't until 2000 that I returned California, this time as a delegate to the Democratic National Convention in LA, and again in 2001 to San Francisco when I was a candidate for the U.S. Senate in Alabama. In 2009, Leslie and I returned to the Bay City area to enjoy Princeton friends and her stepbrothers in Oakland.

But there was much of California left for us to see. Perhaps our biggest omission had been San Diego, with its neighboring picturesque communities of Oceanside, Coronado, and La Jolla. We made up for it on this trip.

We arrived on a one-stop flight to LA on Saturday, June 26, 2021. During the flight I devoured Richard Scrushy's autobiography, *This Shouldn't Happen in America*. After a couple of glitches, we were in our Hertz rental, driving south on the infamous, crowded, six-lane Interstate 5. Our senses were immediately engaged by numerous cars darting back and forth between us and among us. There were multiple opportunities to have an accident. The congested traffic stretched our Oceanside journey to three and a half hours.

Another purpose for this trip was to see Roonie and Richard Landwehr, living in Oceanside for 18 years ever since Richard retired from his Washington, D.C., government building maintenance job. Roonie, then 72, was my dad's secretary in Calcutta, India when he was the American Peace Corps director there, 1967–69. Roonie also helped save my brother David's life in 1970. She was a bridesmaid at Leslie's and my 1974 wedding in Wellesley, Massachusetts. We consider her family, and she certainly is.

Hence this was a special visit with dear friends, savored in the picturesque harbor setting of Oceanside. Earlier I indulged in a late afternoon splashing in the waves of the Pacific Ocean in a neighborhood near our motel.

The next day, Sunday morning, we followed the Landwehrs on a 30-minute drive down Interstate 5 to the beautiful St. Andrew's Episcopal Church in San Diego's northern suburb. The lady priest shared a stimulating sermon. The whole service was uplifting spiritually. I needed it, fed upon it, and afterwards prayed specially with Roonie. I laid my hands on her to alleviate her continued migraine headaches. We also prayed for a desperately needed complete healing.

A few blocks from the church were the beautiful San Diego Botanical

Gardens. Leslie and I enjoyed exploring it, smelling, sniffing, and seeing beautiful flowers. There was also an intriguing diversity of trees from many continents.

We enjoyed the San Diego Heritage Museum across the road. Afterwards we crossed a sky-high bridge to reach Coronado Island, where the U.S. Navy is based. We finally reached the world-famous Coronado Hotel, our destination for the next two nights. What an architectural jewel this picturesque hotel is. It has been in existence since 1888. The majestic Spanish colonial features, its football field-sized courtyard, and its close proximity to the Pacific stimulated our senses and exhilarated our two-day sojourn. The one exception was having my shoes stolen from Coronado Beach while running on the sand near the flapping waves. Another exception was when Leslie, on Monday morning in the underground garage, tripped over a marker, and bruised and bloodied her knee. Bravo to her, rolling as she fell, she still was able to get up and walk. We drove to the San Diego Zoo, where she was patched up at a first-aid station. The zoo lived up to its world-famous reputation, as Leslie and I strolled through its vast grounds, viewing animals from virtually every species. We also rode the buses up and down a maze of streets and alleys, enjoying the upper deck.

The Pacific venues and local cuisine enhanced our journey, both day and night.

On Tuesday morning, June 29, 2021, we rolled off to suburban La Jolla to see the intriguing cliff and waves. With a colony of seals capturing our attention, Leslie's camera was constantly clicking. Late that morning we headed toward San Bernardino and its adjacent national forest. Our ultimate destination was Big Bear Lake.

At Big Bear we enjoyed a rustic cabin (a little less enjoyed by Leslie) and rented a pontoon boat for a two-hour ride on the lake. From a 7,000-foot base altitude we also viewed the 11,000-foot San Gorgonio Mountain. Two days in this gorgeous location were not enough! We bought a beautifully sculpted wooden bear for Grace and family back in Atlanta. It was a family gift for the new baby in their growing brood.

With a schedule ahead of us, we left Big Bear country and drove on Thursday, July 1 to Los Angeles. Our first stop was in the Hollywood

Boulevard area, looking for a Princeton college roommate named Lew Retrum, with whom I had lost touch. We had two old addresses but could not find Lew. We were surprised by two things, however. First, we noticed how many gated blocks existed in residential areas. The second was how many homeless people were sleeping on the sidewalks, far worse than anything seen back home in Alabama. These two surprises were unsurprisingly quite connected.

By mid-afternoon we arrived at the swank yet fairly modern Garland Hotel in the Hollywood neighborhood. This was where the McPhillips wedding party, organized by my brother Frank for his son Dixon, had gathered. Many of us huddled around a favorite nesting place near the pool. It was awesome to see the extended families of my sisters Sandy and Betsy and my brother Frank. My own dear grown children Rachel and Jay Plucker and David and Melinda McPhillips with baby daughter Julia were also present. Joy and light-heartedness sparked the festive mood!

We enjoyed several excursions over the next two days, first to Malibu and Oxnard, and then back to LA, to assist David and Melinda in finding clothes. The second was a July 4 trip to the Griffith Observatory for the bird's eye view of LA. A great rehearsal dinner the preceding Saturday night was hosted by my brother Frank, father of the groom. The final 4th of July wedding in the Malibu Hills was a spectacular event, a thrill for the 120 wedding guests. It was a classic event uniting nephew Dixon and his beautiful bride Katie.

Leslie and I flew back to Atlanta the next morning, July 5. From there we drove back to Montgomery. Daughter Grace, expecting her third, still had not yet delivered. She did so only six days afterwards with a C-Section necessary for a 11-pound, 2-ounce son, "Lucien Grant Lunsford," nicknamed "Luca."

## SOUTH CAROLINA—MY SON ARRIVES

Over the years, our family has enjoyed South Carolina, especially Charleston, in all its glory. We've also visited Columbia, the state capital and home of the University of South Carolina, a repository of Scott and Zelda Fitzgerald archives. We also enjoyed in 2013–2016 watching our son David mature and develop at Anderson University, just across the Georgia line, near Clemson University.

It was my "one and only son," David, who brought us back to the Gamecock State after landing an exciting new job at the Oakbrook Academy in Spartanburg, South Carolina, starting in August 2021.

When the August 23–27, 2021, trial of the three Selma police officers was dismissed by the Alabama attorney general (see Chapter 10), that opened a window for Leslie and me to pop up for three and a half days to the Palmetto State. David, his wife Melinda, and daughter Julia had discovered a nice cottage-like home in Greir, with a charming front porch, halfway between Greenville and Spartanburg, both metropolises. We arrived on Saturday, August 21, in time to catch 10-month-old grandchild Julia McPhillips before her nap. After catching up, David took us all out to the rustic Campbell's Covered Bridge in the foothills of the adjacent North Carolina mountains. That night we feasted on Hibachi food we brought to their house.

The next day began serendipitously with Sunday morning praise and worship on David's front porch, followed by a stimulating TV sermon from Church of the Highlands pastor Chris Hodges. That afternoon David also gave us a personal tour of his new school, Oakbrook, in Spartanburg. Begun in 1992, the private Christian school has an impressive set of five buildings and many state championship trophies. We enjoyed seeing David's classroom where he teaches four religion and two science classes each day to 6th and 7th graders. Our son has even emulated Robin Williams in the famous movie, *Dead Poets Society*, we delightfully learned. That involved standing on top of his desk, to get the kids' attention.

David has a large photograph of Albert Einstein in a poster on the wall behind his desk. David himself has been inspired by this great scientist in several respects, including his wondering mind, his faith in God, and his interest in outer space.

We also enjoyed downtown historic tours of both Spartanburg and Greenville and their developed antique inner cores. We were impressed by Greenville's downtown waterfalls and gardens. That last night we feasted at a picturesque sidewalk restaurant on Main Street.

The next morning, we drove back down to Anderson and observed the progress of the David Larson McPhillips Center for Student Success, so named a year after David's graduation in 2016. We enjoyed the company of certain administrators of the Center, sharing with us how this new program, funded by Leslie and me in David's honor, had helped many Anderson students with learning disabilities.

We didn't get back to South Carolina until a year later. It was on Labor Day weekend, September 2–6, 2022, flying up from Montgomery. Our first stop in a rental car from the Charlotte Airport involved a short drive over to Fort Mills, South Carolina, in Charlotte's suburbs, to have a dinner visit with our long-time dear friends, Mahesh and Bonnie Chavda, world-class healing evangelists. Their conferences at the All-Nations Church in South Carolina are world-famous. Leslie and I have enjoyed them many times over the years. It was also terrific to see their bearded son Ben, an employee in my law office during the summer of 1998. He had evolved into a brilliant business executive for Disney Corporation in Los Angeles. We also enjoyed seeing their daughter Sarah, now her parents' ministry manager. She lived and worked with Leslie and me in Montgomery, active in my 2002 U.S. Senate campaign.

Afterwards we drove down to Grier, South Carolina, to launch a great weekend visit with David, Melinda, and two-year-old Julia, the sixth of our seven grands. What a wonderful rest and recuperation from the rigors of my Montgomery law practice. We shared the season-opening Alabama versus Utah State football game, enjoyed church the next day, and relished Labor Day Monday, despite the unrelenting rain.

## North Carolina—An Awesome State

North Carolina . . . you have always been there, one of the most amazing states in all of America. We all love you, at least here in Alabama.

My first real experience with this awesome state was in the mid-1950s. When I was a nine-year-old, my wonderful maternal grandmother "Stu," as we called her, was based in New Orleans. She also had a summer home in Highlands, North Carolina, and she treated me to Camp Sky Valley in the neighboring mountains. The cold morning skinny-dips in a lake, the outhouses, the hikes up rugged mountains, and the elevated tent barracks, are all lodged forever in my memory from that 1955–56 era.

In the early 1960s, while a cadet at Sewanee Military Academy in neighboring Tennessee, I recall enjoying playing football games in Asheville, North Carolina, against Christ School. Afterwards we toured the sparkling, majestic Biltmore Mansion, more of a castle than a house.

In the 1970s–'80s, Leslie, the kids, and I scooted up to North Carolina on short, quick trips, mostly on long weekends. In the 1995–2003 period, we became increasingly acquainted with the central North Carolina cities of Greensboro, Elon, Raleigh-Durham, and Chapel Hill. During this time first our daughter Rachel, and then our daughter Grace, attended Elon College on its growing, beautiful campus. We enjoyed seeing the area's rapid growth, the campus's enlargement, and the parental experience of enjoying both daughter's college transformation into Elon University. Amazingly Elon has recently leapfrogged other colleges and universities in the *U.S. News and World Report*'s annual ratings.

Leslie and I have also enjoyed the Charlotte area many times, attending spiritual conferences hosted by healing evangelists Michael and Bonnie Chavda during the 1990s–2000s. We also attended the 2012 Democratic National Convention in Charlotte, which renominated Barack Obama. The convention also increased my friendship with future U.S. Senate candidate Cal Cunningham III of Arlington, North Carolina, just up the road from Charlotte.

My dear parents Eleanor and Julian McPhillips also spent much of the 1990s, especially in the milder months, in rustic, beautiful Cashiers in southwestern North Carolina's mountainous terrain. We had wonderful family reunions in and around the incomparable High Hampton Inn, with its 1920s decor and aura, nestled picturesquely in natural architecture.

I also got to know the Outer Banks, that famous peninsula strip of northeastern North Carolina that stretches up into a southeastern segment of Virginia, where my sister Betsy lives in Chesapeake, Virginia, and her daughter Ann, who was recently married to Bill Sleigher.

Thus, on October 8–10, 2021, we all enjoyed a family reunion organized by Leslie in Sapphire, North Carolina, near Cashiers. All three branches of the growing families of Rachel, Grace, and David, including seven grands, were thrilled to celebrate a big birthday consisting of Rachel's 44th, David's 31st, and granddaughter Julia's 1st that weekend.

The drive up to the neighboring mountain stirred many good memories and uplifted our spirits. We rented a house on a steep hill leading down to a creek, and then to Lake Piscataway. The intriguing view from a front deck inspired us to take a trip to Whitewater Falls, roaring in full force from recent rains. This family gathering was a bundle of fun, with great photographs taken—these precious events pass much too rapidly.

## 2022—THE DUTCH ADVENTURE

Planned for two years but COVID-delayed, Leslie and I finally enjoyed a two-week trip to the Netherlands in April 2022.

Organized by Princeton classmate Tom Johnson, twelve of us who graduated in 1968, and an equal number of our ladies, plus one widow and her son, made for a merry traveling band. Two wonderful female guides expanded our numbers to twenty-eight. We caught this beautiful country at its best time of year, the second half of April.

Our group consisted of six doctors, only four fully retired, with two still researching at Harvard Medical School, and one, Dr. Peter Howley, on the cusp of a Nobel Prize for his cancer research discoveries. The doctors included my best friend in the class, retired oncologist Fred Billings of Baton Rouge.

There were four attorneys, only two retired, including Ivy Clubmate Jad Roberts. Still active professionally included organizer Tom Johnson, senior partner in a top Pittsburgh law firm. His most noteworthy case involved suing Saudi Arabia for its role in the infamous 9–11 tragedy that killed 3,000 Americans. Another classmate was San Francisco lawyer John Poggi, by then retired. An Alabama lawyer named McPhillips was still at it. Another formidable attorney was widower Jad Roberts's lady traveling with him, Debby Baum, top litigation attorney in the Winthrop Pillsbury law firm in Washington, D.C., where in 2022, my nephew Jamie McPhillips was working.

There were also two retired business execs, Charlie Byers from Merck, the prescription drug producer extraordinaire, and Mac Lewis, a former IBM exec who started his own computer company.

The diversity was enhanced by our wives, including still active Dr. Susan Gloyd, the life partner of classmate Dr. Bill Gloyd, both of New Mexico, with practices including many Native Americans. The camaraderie and fellowship among our travelers added to the joy of seeing new and wonderful sights.

Bicycles were everywhere. Dodging them was an art form we soon learned—the average Dutchman, at least in the Amsterdam area, had up to three bicycles. Walking and dodging were our main mode of transportation, aided by buses for longer distances.

During our first afternoon in Amsterdam, before everyone else arrived, Leslie and I enjoyed a "Handel's Messiah" bravo performance. The orchestra and singers were "bravissimo." The audience was overwhelmingly maskless, unconcerned about Covid. Spilling outside afterwards we traipsed around Museum Park, resembling Central Park, New York. Clusters of people were spread out on blankets, eating a meal, napping, or throwing frisbees. Musical groups chimed in, while protest groups were raising cain about the Russian invasion of Ukraine, as well as the Turkish invasion of Kurdistan. It felt like the "Vietnam protest" era in America of the late 1960s. Conversation with total strangers was spontaneous, adding to the fun.

The picturesque canals and stores, some architectural gems, made the walking distance worth it. All those miles made our feet and legs sore, as our senior ages were kicking in. This was true whether we admitted it or not.

The art of Dutch masters is second to none. We enjoyed the Van Gogh Museum and the Rijksmuseum, with spectacular collections of the works of Rembrandt, Vermeer, Reubens, Peeters, Hals, Potter, Steen, Bruegel, and many others.

I was moved deeply emotionally by both the Dutch National Resistance Museum and the Dutch Holocaust Memorial. The latter contained the names of 110,000 Jews and other persecuted and killed by the Nazis during World War II. Later the Anne Frank Museum reduced me to tears.

All that "hiding in the attic" harsh conditions of life for this young teenage girl and her family, captured late in the war, and sent to Auschwitz. Only her father survived but he went back, and found her diary, and made it world-famous.

Most of the trip was on a more joyous note. On our third day we absorbed the spectacular Keukenhof Gardens, walking through 300 different types of tulips, blazing in every color under the sun. Leslie's favorite, the "Nightmare," was a deep purple, almost black. Climbing an ancient 75-foot-high windmill in the gardens gave us an exalted view of the grounds.

Holland is known for its windmills. In Kinderdijk we saw numerous large 1730s-era Dutch windmills, towering at least 100 feet, while sucking up and replacing high levels of water, to suit the lowlands' needs.

We also enjoyed an 1890s Dutch sailing ship and a local woodchopper's humorous presentation of how to make wooden shoes. We reveled in seeing Dutch Cheesemaking in Gouda. We also enjoyed the production of Royal Delph China in the city of the same name, Delph.

The first half of the trip we were in the Pulitzer Hotel in Amsterdam. The second half was at Hotel Des Indes in The Hague, the legislative capital of the Netherlands. That location provided easy access to Leiden, the ancient Dutch capital from which early pilgrims immigrated to America.

Another incredible highlight was a visit to the Peace Palace, a spectacularly impressive castle built 1913–1916 with Andrew Carnegie's money. Among other worldwide peace-making functions it plays, it also houses the International Court of Justice. This august body has mediated many boundary line disputes and trade issues between nations but has frustratingly been denied the opportunity to tame the Russian invasion of Ukraine.

A highlight for Leslie and me, mid-trip, was a visit to The Hague from our daughter Rachel, husband Jay, and their three children, Laurel, Jude, and Sage, our precious grands. They drove over from Wiesbaden, Germany where Jay was stationed with the U.S. Army Corps of Engineers. Another pleasant surprise was contact in Amsterdam by our nephew Dixon McPhillips, my brother Frank's youngest son.

We dodged Covid, with a negative testing required within 24 hours of our return flight to the USA. Among our co-travelers, 15 of 26 tested positive, but without symptoms, probably due to their vaccinations. They required hastily written letters from our "group docs" enabling them to return to America without quarantining. By then, we were safely back home.

This great trip was psychologically, if not physically, restful, and parts were thrilling. In the end, fellow traveler Fred Billings described the journey "as near perfect as it could be," and Leslie and I agreed.

## DENMARK/GREENLAND ESCAPADE

Three months after returning from Holland, Leslie and I set out in July, extending our travels to Denmark and Greenland. This was not a retiree trip and at times was rugged. It was the second segment, however, of sabbatical leave promised long ago to my sweetheart of 49 years.

We arrived in Denmark on July 4, 2022, a big day for America, but a different occasion in this ancient land of the Vikings, and more modern-day savvy Europeans.

At 75 and 74 respectively, we are "no spring chickens," to use one of my favorite phrases. Our energy levels are usually sufficient but occasionally were tested by all the walking in both Denmark and Greenland. The afternoon we arrived we saw the famous "Little Mermaid" statue in Copenhagen's harbor. The next day we enjoyed the National Museum, soaking up the Viking culture and history. Captivating also was the Copenhagen Museum, with its portrayal of the city's culture from the 1500s onward. Especially interesting was all the history on Danish theologian-philosopher Soren Kierkegaard, long one of my favorites in the field. The palaces, parks, and museums (one sponsoring an exhibit on Neanderthal man and other earliest human ancestors) were fascinating. So also, was the Danish Resistance Museum, depicting the Danes' historic fight against the Nazis.

On our fourth day, we flew to Greenland for a week. That land has the look of early pioneer days of America. The native "Inuit" share an ancestry of Mongolian origin, coming from over the Bering Strait 10,000 years ago, into Northern Canada and Alaska, and filtering down into Greenland. In 1000–1200, the Norsemen and Vikings also poured in. They only stayed in Greenland for a couple of centuries, before retreating, returning again in the 1500s–1700s. The only inhabitable parts of Greenland, the world's largest island, are the eastern and western coastlines, especially the side closer to northern Canada.

We arrived by Greenland Airlines from Copenhagen, on July 8, 2022, flying into Kangerlussuaq, a town of 4,000 people. We then flew south to the more industrious town of Nuuk, with a population of 19,000, and the legislative capital since 2009. From there, we boarded an orange-colored ferry boat with modest but comfortable cabins. The two-day cruise up the coast was picturesque and exhilarating.

Thus, we arrived in Ilulissat, midway up the western coast, and home of unbelievably beautiful glaciers, icebergs, and whales surfacing for camera-ready pictures. We were the only Americans in our mostly Danish group of 15, which included a Swedish couple and a German man. One day's six-mile hike up and down rocky boulders and slippery sod, juxtaposed to breathtaking glaciers, taxed our senior bodies, but delighted our souls.

After a week soaking in this Artic beauty and history, we flew back to Denmark and rented a car. We drove from Copenhagen through Zealand to the middle Danish province of Fyn, and visited Odense, the hometown of Hans Christian Andersen. This Danish writer is the world-renowned author of fairytales for children. Learning more about his story in a world-class museum was a true highlight of the trip.

In closing, I recommend travel as a great fantastic/wonderful/terrific way to discover new and innovative ideas, new people, and new worlds. It is my hope to continue to travel as long as I can. It is a way to grow in Spirit and sometimes in our last lives. It is all worth the effort.

Travel is an adventure that is in our blood. We are not alone as this wanderlust is also shared by many of our friends. We have discovered, not surprisingly, that there are always others who prefer to stay much closer to home. We of course respect that.

We hope to live a long life and make many more trips, as much as time, our good health, and budget will allow. As for the present, we are staying closer to home as health and family responsibilities have slowed us down.

# 6

# 'Dead Weight' Takes on Her Accuser

Kwonethia Boswell, 38, and husband Paul Boswell Jr. first came to see me on August 29, 2019. I represented her father-in-law, the late Reverend Paul Boswell Sr., in 2003 when he pastored the People's Baptist Church. That year I filed suit against political boss Joe Reed and Alabama State University, fighting their attempt to condemn by eminent domain the church and its surrounding block, to grab the land for a "state use" expansion by ASU. My lawsuit caused a quadrupling of the $125,000 offered by ASU to the church, bumping it up to $500,000. The church could not move elsewhere. Most unfortunately, a few years later a mentally ill person murdered Paul Boswell Sr.

Against this backdrop I enthusiastically welcomed the Boswells 16 years later. Kwonethia (nicknamed "Neat"), was strongly supported by Paul Jr. I sympathized with her dismay about the way her employer Auburn University had treated her in her employment as a counselor of students in its clinical psychology program. Armed with both a master's degree and PhD in psychology from the University of Mississippi, Boswell began working for Auburn University in August 2007. She quickly developed a good rapport with the students she was counseling. That made her popular in the African American community. Yet with older Caucasians, problems unfortunately developed.

When Kwonethia first began working at Auburn, no requirement existed that she be a "licensed psychologist" to perform her clinical work as a student counselor. The man who hired her, Dr. Doug Hankes became "deliberately hurtful" towards her, Boswell repeated this to the Equal Employment Opportunity Commission (EEOC) in Birmingham in 2019.

Said Boswell about Hankes: "He is belittling me by stating that I am 'dead weight' in the Student Counseling division of the Psychological

Services Department."

"He further demeaned me," said Kwonethia, "when Dr. Hankes told my supervisor Dr. Jan Miller, she was wasting an hour of her time each week supervising [me]." Boswell believed she had always gotten along well with Miller. She was working hard, including many extra hours. And the students loved her, she said.

It sounded like bullying was going on, with a racial twist. Boswell said in her EEOC charge: "I also could not help but note, when hired, that I was the only African American senior staff clinician in the Department at that time, as opposed to eight Caucasian clinicians within the Department."

Auburn is in great need of African American students desiring a counselor from a similar demographic background, Boswell added. Some of her best counselees at Auburn were Caucasian or international students from a diversity of backgrounds. "I am committed to inclusion and diversity," Boswell insisted to the EEOC.

A different mindset and mood existed among her supervisors.

While Auburn University in principle is committed to equal opportunity, especially with so many great black athletes and a black athletic director. Nonetheless, many professors on campus have said Auburn is "the whitest school in the SEC." They are referring to the Southeastern Conference, stated sportswriter Joseph Goodman of the *Birmingham News*, citing statistics in a March 2021 column.

Her EEOC charge states, "Dr. Hankes definitely did not treat his white student counselors so disrespectfully as he treated me." Boswell added that the "sum total . . ." was a cold and hostile work environment, . . . pervasive and distressing."

As my representation of Boswell developed, I associated attorney Tanika Finney, of counsel to us at McPhillips Shinbaum, to help me analyze the strengths and weaknesses of this case. She did excellent work. Of the same gender and ethnicity as Kwonethia, Finney injected insight and credibility to advice given this client.

During the last four months of 2019 and 2020, we navigated Covid. Communications were primarily through the EEOC. Nonetheless, we kept the pressure on Auburn, Boswell seriously considered a lawsuit.

Finally, in December 2020, we ironed out an agreement restoring her sense of well-being. She signed confidential papers acknowledging the matter was "resolved by mutual agreement." Proud to have stood up to those who bullied her, Kwonethia Boswell, mask on face, left to pursue the next of her life at a more receptive location. It was my honor to have helped her along the way.

# 7

# Lee County Sheriff's Justice Lacking

On May 11, 2018, former Auburn football player Kwesi Drake, all six feet two inches and 320 pounds of him, looking as solid as granite, came to see me. How could anyone his size ever be bullied by anyone? Not physically to be sure, but legally he was vulnerable. After all he was Black.

The office of sheriff in any Alabama county carries with it many privileges. Sheriff Jay Jones of Lee County was no exception, and he was indisputably Caucasian. He believed he could do no wrong.

What's wrong with stocking his jails with black correctional officers? Sheriff Jones considered this the "Correctional side" of his office, where blacks are most needed, while whites dominated the "Enforcement side" of his office. Their work was more outdoors, and in contact with the public.

I helped Drake prepare an EEOC charge to file in Birmingham on May 11, 2018. After the US Justice Department reviewed it, we received a right to sue letter. It took 12 and a half months or until May 28, 2019.

After football, Drake spent his senior year at Auburn interning with the Lee County Sheriff's Office. He realized his passion was in law enforcement and expressed this to Sheriff Jones, who deemed it necessary for Kwesi to first go to a correctional job. That was in 2002. Yet, the persistent Kwesi finally landed in 2003 in a patrol division job as a sheriff's deputy.

Drake applied in 2004 for the coveted investigator's job, his ultimate goal. He interviewed for an open job posting and was informed he had outscored everyone during the testing. Kwesi was highly recommended for the job by Captain Van Jackson, the top-ranked African American in the office. Sadly, Drake learned that Sheriff Jones gave the job to a Caucasian who was not recommended for the post.

Drake finally landed an investigator's job and held that for the next 14 years. He actually became a star investigator, helping the office make many big cases.

In 2010, when the opportunity developed, Drake applied for an Investigative Sergeant's position, and outscored his competitors for the job. The promotion went instead to a Caucasian female, much less qualified by all objective standards and test scores.

The "apply and deny" process kept repeating itself for opportunities that should have been Drake's. His talents frequently helped the Sheriff's Office resolve difficult cases, especially in the black community. His ethnicity was actually an asset in resolving cases.

The foot-dragging reluctance of Sheriff Jones toward Drake "appeared solely motivated by his race," said Drake in his lawsuit filed on August 12, 2019. The Lee County Sheriff's Office was divided into two primary divisions, Corrections and Enforcement. The Enforcement division had approximately 200 officers. That included only four blacks constituting only 2 percent of the workforce in a county with a 25 percent black population. A disproportionately higher number of blacks interacted with the Lee County Sheriff's Office, voluntarily or involuntarily.

In an analytical lawsuit, revised several times by Drake himself, we alleged a "good old boy" system dominating the Lee County Sheriff's Office. It led to blatant race discrimination by combining the two different divisions, Enforcement and Corrections, into a modern-day Apartheid. The goal was to keep black deputies out of public sight with limited public interaction. Of the 86 sworn deputy sheriffs in the Enforcement Division, only six were African American.

Drake's lawsuit addressed the convoluted maze of interactions that kept the Lee County Sheriff's Office segregated within its two divisions.

As time zoomed by in the Covid Era, from March 2020 onward, we kept scheduling the deposition of the Sheriff. It was canceled, reset, and then postponed again. Finally, mediation with the legendary Phil Adams of Opelika helped us resolve the case. On December 11, 2020, with co-counsel Tanika Finney's assistance, we met and resolved this great dispute.

Drake is bound by confidentiality provisions from saying anything more. I am confident his lawsuit, and even the mere filing of his suit, before finally going to court, influenced the hiring of more blacks in the Enforcement division. These hirings were designed to counter our suit. Drake believed a more progressive day for racial justice in Lee County would be coming. If so, it will positively impact the dynamic cities of Auburn and Opelika, and other more rural sites in Alabama.

Thanks be to God that people like Kwesi Drake have the courage and integrity to stand up to institutional bullies. Progress often comes in bits and pieces. However, this was a leap forward over institutional racism.

# 8

# Wile E. Coyote-Esque Hyundai Crash

Hyundai Motor Corporation is the third-largest automobile manufacturer in the world, and its plant in Montgomery, Alabama, is
its primary American operation. When Montgomery landed the Korean
automaker in 2003, it was considered a huge victory by the Alabama Governor. Montgomery's Chamber of Commerce was grinning from ear to
ear as Alabama defeated several other Southern states in bagging Hyundai.

Yet, somewhere along the way, beginning with Alabama's waiver of
multiple millions of taxes, Hyundai developed an arrogance. It acted like
America's labor and employment laws did not apply to it. Hyundai quickly
developed a climate of insensitivity, routinely allowing but then denying claims of race, sex, age, and disability discrimination. The worst was
Hyundai's running over one of the most heroic but humble workers I have
known. He was a blue-collar genius named Mike Keller. It also helped
significantly to have the brilliant federal judge Myron Thompson issue a
historic and literary opinion, denying summary judgment for Hyundai.

So, what actually happened? How did it start? It was a massacre on
March 8, 2018, when the 50-year-old Keller and 20 other mostly senior
employees, without warning, were suddenly terminated. Eighteen of the
twenty-one employees "restructured out" of Hyundai were over 40 years
of age, and most were over 50. Of the other three employees, barely under
40, only one had a serious health problem. Hyundai rid itself of all in one
fell swoop.

Caught so unexpectedly, the 20 employees besides Keller soon caved
into financial pressure, accepting modest payouts in exchange for their
legal rights and releasing all claims against Hyundai, while agreeing to
non-disparagement of the company. Keller was offered $22,000, but he
quickly turned the offer down. Another unusual feature required each

recipient of Hyundai's money to agree never to testify against Hyundai. Arguing public policy, and knowing that this was unconscionable, we persuaded a federal magistrate judge to convince Hyundai this was an invalid witness restraint, at least for Keller's then-pending lawsuit.

So, who really was and is this Mike Keller? This group leader of Hyundai's Stamping Division was a creative genius, whatever the color of his collar was. Keller's 69 inventions saved or made Hyundai millions of dollars over the years. Just after Hyundai opened its Montgomery plant in 2005, Keller's picture was twice featured in *Time* magazine cover stories. Keller was the only Hyundai employee pictured in either story. What an honor!

So why terminate Keller? Classic "Age Discrimination" was rearing its ugly head, and this was proven in federal court.

After two years of legal discovery, including interrogatories and depositions, Hyundai filed a motion for summary judgment in early August 2020, backed by a myriad of documents, high-paid attorneys, and a $535 per hour expert witness. Knowing what was at stake, our trio of attorneys—David Sawyer, Chase Estes, and I—put together an impressive counter brief filed on September 2, 2020. Finally, five months later, Judge Thompson issued a 39-page opinion, gutting Hyundai's age discrimination defense, as he poetically wrote, "Hyundai's argument crashes, Wile E. Coyote-esque, into veritable mountains of contrary precedent."

In rejecting the auto manufacturer's defense against age discrimination, Judge Thompson added another lyrical touch, saying Hyundai's position was "cutting the bacon too thin."

Thompson's January 19, 2021, opinion was the successful result of almost three years of Mike Keller's fighting against the corporate giant that wrongfully bullied him and 20 other dedicated workers at its Montgomery plant. Keller the Giant Killer had prevailed against a Goliath corporation!

IGNORING STRONG EVIDENCE OF age discrimination, Hyundai's original 2018 offer to Keller, was hardly satisfactory to a man making $140,000 annually with good benefits, after 14 years of working his tail off, night and day. Moreover, no other vehicle manufacturing jobs were available near Montgomery if Keller desired to remain with his wife, mother, and daughters. This was absolutely his wish. Other Alabama auto manufacturing jobs were in Tuscaloosa, Huntsville, or Anniston, too far away for daily travel. And no Alabama car plant would want Keller anyway after he had dared sue Hyundai. Hence, Keller courageously rejected the severance package.

What was Keller's experience on March 8, 2018, the day of the massacre? It started much like any other day, as he was seated in his cubicle preparing for a familiar morning meeting. Department head Mike McCabe and assistant manager Chris Boysen arrived and stood near Keller's cubicle in an ominous manner. It was 5:50 a.m. and the meeting he was preparing for was to begin in ten minutes. Without explanation, McCabe asked Keller to walk to the administrative building, informing him that Boysen could lead the day's morning meeting. Keller sensed that something was afoot. Once they arrived at administration, he could overhear talk about different rooms being set up. The atmosphere was tense and Keller couldn't comprehend why, but he knew he was being terminated.

He was ushered into one of the empty meeting rooms where he sat at a small table, McCabe to his right and Delicia McIntyre from Human Resources to his left. The door remained open. Keller could see that Scott Gordy of Human Resources was standing outside the door observing and listening. The unmistakably rehearsed speech began. McIntyre spoke firmly and without emotion, as she got straight to the point. Without explanation, she stated that his employment was terminated and asked for him to turn over any company keys, phones, corporate cards, and PPE in his possession. Then, she went straight into sharing the highlights of the severance package sitting before her on the table, namely the $22,000, as if it were a spoon of cough syrup that would magically make this stunning turn of events palatable.

McIntyre was interrupted by Keller several times as he asked over and over, "Who put my name in the hat?" His persistence began to erode McIntyre's rehearsed composure. Gordy, still outside the door, could see that she'd been thrown off her game, no longer poised to stay on script. Keller could see Gordy frantically waving his arms. Finally, McIntyre saw him. By then her voice was beginning to crack and mid-sentence, in her exasperation, she blurted out, "Which door do you want to go out?" He simply replied, "What difference does it make as long as I can get to my truck."

At this point, McCabe, who'd been friendly to him over the years, intervened and stated that he would escort Keller out. They stood up, and walked the few steps outside the room where Keller extended his hand to Gordy, who'd been just outside. He accepted the gesture, seemingly offering Keller a consoling handshake. At this, the security guard, clearly present to intimidate and control the massacre, lunged towards the men. McCabe quickly stated, "Calm down, they are just shaking hands!" As the men walked, McCabe apologized to Keller, further sharing that he couldn't believe what was happening. Keller would relive this morning again and again. It would haunt his thoughts and spawn disturbing dreams. He had post-traumatic stress for some time.

Ever the dutiful and conscientious employee, before Keller left the parking lot that day, he sent a text to McCabe and Boysen. He wanted to make certain they knew that the TMA tooling hangers were complete, and the large LP-gas bottle was full for the 120 forklifts. That was the last text he sent. However, for an entire year, he would be included in all upper management group text correspondence.

The termination took a considerable emotional toll on Keller. After 14 years with Hyundai, not only did he take considerable personal pride in being a part of the organization, but as a group leader he endeavored to cultivate the same with his peers and in his team. He supported his colleague Daryl Sanders's idea to repaint and clean up, while Sanders supported his safety and modification initiative in scrap chute production, floor production, and safety. After seeing several near misses that could have ended in catastrophe, Sanders knew from experience that Keller's insight and improvement efforts in these areas were always worthy of pursuing.

The beautification endeavor was a two-month campaign they dubbed "Bringing Back the Pride." This initiative was designed to cultivate a sense of ownership and instill pride in the staff by involving them in the process of making aesthetic improvements to their respective workstations. Both men both purchased paint out of their own pockets and assisted in these efforts on their days off, leading by example. Ironically, after at the conclusion of this cheerful endeavor, Keller was unceremoniously and harshly removed from the premises that were his second home.

After a sleepless night, Keller rose to stare at his phone. While waiting to place a call to human resources, he reflected on his career at Hyundai. His mind was spinning as the previous fourteen years replayed in his mind. Nothing could reconcile the sad and unexpected end.

As he recalled the value he'd brought to the organization from the day he was hired, he thought of having been the first-hired and the longest-serving employee in the stamping shop. His recommendations also led to dozens of additional hires for the new plant's opening. He considered his contributions, his loyalty, and the value Hyundai had seemingly placed in sending him for multiple training courses at Auburn University and Trenholm Tech over the years. He thought about the many senior managers he'd personally trained. Keller had even been one of the rare worldwide Hyundai employees to receive the Global Quality Achievement Award of Excellence.

Keller had set up all of the production processes and made modifications throughout the shop, saving the company millions. He was selected to represent the Montgomery plant, traveling to both Japan and South Korea to train and show off his inventions to other Hyundai manufacturing locations so they too could benefit from his innovations. In the South Korea home office, his framed *Time* magazine page was literally taken down from an executive's wall for him to sign. He was recognized and treated like a Hyundai superstar.

Over these years, his compassion and congeniality also spoke volumes about his character. Countless times he'd prepared food for the staff— rib luncheons, burger cookouts, and such—often at his personal expense. He'd attended 13 funerals in 14 years, the only manager who could make such a claim of worker support. And now, he sat in his home wondering how this company that he'd saved millions of dollars had shown him the door with a parting offer of $22,000. Where was the respect, compassion, or humanity he knew in his heart that he'd earned?

About 8:30 the day after dismissal, he called HMMA to speak to Delicia McIntyre in Human Resources. She had been the person to deliver the previous morning's distressing news, firmly and coldly terminating his employment. Her tone was notably different from the day before, as she sounded utterly pleased to receive his defeated call. He was feeling lost and initially inquired as to the process to receive the measly severance package. She asked if he would hold briefly, but then failed to properly place him on hold! For Keller, this was a moment of pure serendipity. He could hear that her fingers had tapped a button, but as fate would have it, it was the wrong one. McIntyre apparently had no idea that Keller was listening to her insensitive and clumsy statement to the room that, "Mr. Keller is on the phone right now. He's wanting his money! He's ready to sign the severance agreement. It's not going to be as difficult as we thought!" To Keller's complete shock and dismay, he heard loud cheers in the room as if the home team had just scored the winning touchdown. He realized the HR people were not only doing Hyundai's dirty work, they were enthralled by it. He could hardly believe his ears as he collapsed in his chair in disbelief. He could hear her attempt to quiet the room before she again blundered with the hold button, then thinking she was taking him off hold. Her stunning, unprofessional and callous moment planted a seed that would grow to ultimately lead Keller to my law offices to initiate the biggest fight of his life. He was ready to stand up to this corporate bully, in part with thanks due to McIntyre's clumsy fingers. For Keller, this was divine intervention.

Hyundai's initial forty-five-day deadline for Keller to sign the severance agreement passed without his cooperation. It was increased to one hundred days, during which nothing changed. By this point, it was clear that Mike Keller wasn't amenable to the severance agreement. Soon after, Rick Neal, Hyundai's head legal counsel since 2003, resigned and moved to Georgia.

Keller spent March to June 2018 in a quandary. Frequently depressed by the undeserved unfairness, he remained unrelenting. Hyundai had been his family for many years. He had given the auto manufacturer his blood, sweat, tears, and unwavering loyalty, helping to make it tons of money. Keller's loyalty was not reciprocated by Hyundai, which didn't see it as a two-way street. Hyundai would learn the hard way the price of such arrogance.

KELLER, NOT KNOWING ANY better, first visited the established Montgomery law firms of Rushton, Stakely; Ball, Ball & Duke; and Capell & Howard. Their corporate-minded attorneys quickly turned him away, informing Keller that he "didn't have a case," and should "take his $22,000 and run, while it was still on the table."

By June 8, 2018, Keller had heard about me, and he telephoned for an appointment. Three days later he gave me his strong but sad-ending Hyundai history. Initially Keller considered his firing to be due to something else six years earlier. I informed him that the time period for filing suit had long since run out on any such issues. I smelled there was much more at issue and discerned that age discrimination was likely involved. In fact, it seemed obvious, since 18 of the 21 who were let go were over 40 years old. Most, like Keller, were over 50. By June 26, I had prepared and filed a charge of age discrimination for Keller against Hyundai, to recover damages. I sent an advance copy of the charge with a cover letter to top company officials. No response came from them. Soon, however, Birmingham attorney Michael Lucas of the distinguished Burr Forman law firm contacted me as Hyundai's representative.

Once charges are filed with the Equal Employment Opportunity Commission (EEOC) in Birmingham, as we did in June 2018, the matter can rock on for months before one receives the all-important "right to sue" letter from the EEOC. Meanwhile, Mike Keller was contacting me almost daily, by email or telephone with ideas, opinions, and witnesses. When we finally received a right-to-sue on March 4, 2019, we wasted no time in filing suit on March 22. Courtesy calls to corporate counsel accomplished nothing. Thus, the battle sprung forward. Swords were drawn.

The "discovery process," by which both sides learn about the other side's facts, continued in earnest for the next two years. Hyundai attorneys Michael Lucas and Meryl Cowan deluged us with several thousand pages of "Bates Stamped" documents. Most were designed to send us down irrelevant rabbit holes. Given this clever avoidance, we filed motions to require

Hyundai to produce necessary information.

At one point, I said to client Keller that an age discrimination expert could help us. On his own initiative, Keller got on the Internet and discovered Dr. Linnda Durre of Winter Haven, Florida, a highly energetic 72-year-old with the energy of a 27-year-old. She soon joined our team, despite my reservations about her age, expertise, and credentials. She proved very helpful, lighting a fire under us about the historic significance of Keller's case.

When Keller was first terminated, his HOD (Head of Department), Michael McCabe, loudly remarked that Keller's termination was "not-performance-related." The unhappy McCabe disagreed strongly with the termination. He would repeat what higher management told him, namely that it was a "restructuring," or a "reduction in force." The assistant managers who ranked just above Keller's group leader position, namely Daryl Sanders and Soohong Kim, had both been trained by Keller. Both confirmed in depositions their great unhappiness about Keller's wrongful termination. Both insisted that Keller taught them everything they knew about stamping. He was a dynamic group leader indeed.

As time progressed, Keller kept sending into my office various co-workers, mostly still at Hyundai. All sang his praises, contradicting newly offered Hyundai reasons that Keller's termination was due to "low productivity" and "low morale." A total of 25 co-employees eventually came to my office, often without notice. They were crowding my schedule, but giving me one affidavit after another.

One such employee, 62-year-old LaMorris Heard, stated under oath, in paragraphs 2–6 of his affidavit of October 21, 2019:

2. It is my desire to help set the record straight about certain things attributed to former employee Mike Keller, apparently by higher management.

3. I have seen a Restructuring Recommendation form prepared by Hyundai Motor Manufacturing of Alabama that purports to give a Performance Management Review score for former employee Mike Keller. It states in a rectangular blank about Mr. Keller that:

"Lowest PDRs for Stamping Group leaders since 2012.

Not self-sufficient; requires constant supervision.

Lacks respect from his subordinates."

4. The above-quoted comment is absolutely inaccurate. I was in the same stamping group at HMMA that Mike Keller was in, and I have worked with Mr. Keller for 14½ years. Mr. Keller has always had the highest respect among his fellow co-workers. His leadership ability inspired us all to work harder for Hyundai. His attention to detail and his care for his fellow workers increased our efficiencies around the press area and caused us to work safer and produce better parts. Mr. Keller required no supervision, and to my knowledge, Mr. Keller helped train many of the management over him.

Heard added:

5. Moreover, his counterpart, Bill Carter, who was chosen to be kept as a group leader rather than Mr. Keller, would have been a more logical choice for termination, based on his performance, discipline issues, and true lack of respect from his subordinates.

6. I also have seen Hyundai's Supplemental Response to Plaintiff's consolidated Discovery Requests to Defendant, and particularly the Defendant's Response to Interrogatory No. 2. I particularly take great issue with the following answer:

. . . Furthermore, the morale in Mr. Keller's area was very low, and this low morale was leading to additional problems and concerns among his team members.

. . . On the contrary, Mr. Keller helped raise and maintain morale among his team members. With Mr. Keller's being forced out, the morale is now lower than ever. It's like no one listens to the employees anymore. We are just a name.

Similar words were expounded in two dozen other affidavits from Hyundai workers. These strong rebuttals of Hyundai's position blew me away. Mike Keller was extraordinarily missed by almost all of Hyundai's co-employees! And this was a vast understatement for those who knew Keller best.

Reflecting Keller's compassion for his co-workers, he was the only Hyundai representative who attended the funerals of Black co-employees' family funerals. He did it many times.

Other Hyundai employees were equally exuberant about Keller: One said, "Mike Keller was a hardworking guy everyone loved . . . we would all love to have him back." Plant employee Cedric Martin added: "Mike Keller ran the stamping shop productively, without any supervision and was responsible for many improvements, including better morale."

Former HMMA team leader Mitchell Turner said, "Mike (Keller) was very diligent in finding all VINS with possible defects. The fact that HMMA sent Keller to find defects with his attention to detail confirms that HMMA trusted Keller to protect the customer, as well as them."

It often occurred to me that in terminating Mike Keller, HMMA didn't just shoot itself in the foot. It shot itself in the head. Hyundai totally lacked common sense in firing him, and its bullying Keller and the others backfired on it big time! Civil justice had asserted itself.

Keller was humble and dedicated. More than that, he truly was a caring and respected leader. After his termination, thirty-seven former employees and colleagues voluntarily took the time to offer affidavits and/or letters of support; most were still employed at Hyundai. To the very end of his employment, he was always thinking of ways to make things better on multiple fronts. Right before his termination, he'd developed a less complicated and more accurate vacation scheduling calendar that Team Relations wanted him to train other department leaders to utilize. His creative spirit was appreciated, and his absence was noted by many who appreciated him. His peers and employees were as dumbfounded by his termination as he was.

NOT UNTIL ALMOST TWO years after filing the initial EEOC charge, on January 23, 2020, did Hyundai's lawyers take Mike Keller's deposition. We also deposed HMMA senior managers Craig Stapley, Robert Burns, and Jeff Parrott. The next day, I took the depositions of Hyundai middle managers Soohong Kim and Daryl Sanders, and top executive Chris Susock.

These depositions could not have gone better for Keller. At the end,

Hyundai's mid-manager Sanders confirmed he felt threatened by Hyundai in giving his deposition. That caused defense lawyer Michael Lucas to jump up at the deposition table, and angrily wag his finger at me, screaming, "You'll regret that," adding that he might file a motion in court. I replied, "Go ahead; we'll file our own motion." Guess what? Lucas never filed any motion, nor did I, at least on that issue.

The most amazing thing coming out of these depositions was that suddenly Hyundai executives changed their story for a third time. They spun a yarn about a new rationale for terminating Keller. Top executives Stapley and Susock sputtered for the first time that, "Mike Keller was not anti-union enough for HMMA" and "Keller didn't do enough to discourage potential union organizing."

No hint of this had been stated before by Hyundai anywhere.

The executives could not produce a single shred of evidence of pro-union activities by Keller. This was just their made-up opinion. The only other group leader in the Stamping Department when Keller was terminated, namely Bill Carter, had a much worse discipline record. At 37, he was 13 years younger than Keller. Additionally, Zack Morris, the group leader replacing Keller, was also 37. He had virtually no prior experience in the intricate art of stamping, and no experience in Hyundai's operations.

Based on these flat-out statements under oath by top Hyundai managers, we amended our federal complaint to allege state law violations due to Hyundai's anti-union activities.

The excellent Burr Forman defense team of veteran Michael Lucas and seasoned Meryl Cowan fought back hard, laying it on thick in a long summary judgment brief accompanied by many deposition excerpts, documents, charts, and expert witness proclamations. Well assisted by co-counsel Chase Estes and David Sawyer, we fired off an excellent brief in return, filing it on September 2, 2020.

In assembling our Opposition Response, Mike Keller came to my Lake Martin retreat three different weekends, to help us prepare his case.

Especially helpful to Keller's strategy and game plan was former H.R. Manager, Linda Cook, 61, then living in Pennsylvania. I called her many times, but she always gave me a bucketful of information. Four senior

H.R. managers were among the massacred members. The oldest was Pat Adams, 69, fighting cancer and much in need of the health insurance she lost when she was fired in the midst of treatment. Although she spoke with me several times, she died in the middle of Keller's three-year fight, cheering for us.

Another very helpful member of the 21 massacred was Stephen Guy, 53 years old. After looking for work locally, and with all the OEM automotive plants in the southeast, having used up his severance and all of his 401K, he moved to Cullman. He had finally found a job working for a medical device manufacturer. Guy outlined the strong correlation between age and those exercising their Family Medical Leave Act (FMLA) status.

Unfortunately for these 20 other senior employees, at least three also filed EEOC complaints or naively signed away their right to contest their terminations in return for inadequate compensation.

Months passed, and finally on December 14, 2020, Judge Myron Thompson placed a telephone conference call to all five lawyers involved. It blew me away when defense lawyer Meryl Cowan said to the judge that Mike Keller was "the least productive employee ever at Hyundai." I said to myself, "How could this guy, whose 69 inventions helped save Hyundai millions be the least productive? What dream world do they live in?" I could hardly control my response, and actually my favorite judge snapped back at me for speaking a little out of turn. Maybe I deserved it, but no harm was done yet.

On January 19, 2021, Judge Thompson issued a majestic opinion, denying summary judgment for Hyundai. He also hit the company hard. The court had disagreed with its "but for" arguments against age discrimination.

After this ruling, Judge Thompson telephoned us all in a joint conference. He strongly urged us to settle the case. He recommended the mediation services of U.S. Magistrate Judge Jerusha Adams. We were too far apart. That effort did not succeed. The fight continued.

Given Keller's lost wages, health insurance, and retirement benefits, minus a small credit to Hyundai for the little Keller earned in his bee-keeping business, we estimated his present losses were at least half a million.

If willfulness in age discrimination were proven, and we, his attorneys, considered that highly provable, then his damages would double to $1 million. We added $300,000 in attorney fees for three years' worth of three attorneys and multiple paralegals working together well-documented hundreds of hours. We projected future lost wages for the next 12 years to be close to $2.2 million. Hence our initial position was that Hyundai owed Mike Keller $3.5 million. And that's all I can properly say.

THIS IS BIG! WE also challenged Hyundai by showing them its 2018 Human Rights policy statement, "specifically excluding age" as a protected demographic that Hyundai would not discriminate against. This policy covered everything else: race, sex, national origin, religion, etc. Other key evidence against Hyundai also popped up. We were eager and ready to try this case.

The spring of 2021 passed quickly, as we headed for trial on June 7, 2021. Surprisingly and unfortunately for us, two weeks before that date, Judge Thompson recused to allow himself more time to address Alabama's burgeoning prison crisis. A brand-new judge was appointed, only recently elevated by the Trump administration, namely Corey Mase, 42 years old and a member of the Federalist Society. The trial was rescheduled for October 18, 2021. Throughout the summer of 2021, the case stagnated as direct negotiations remained unproductive. We all speculated about Judge Mase.

In September 2021, Mike Keller, his attorneys, and Hyundai and its attorneys finally agreed to end this epic dispute. We further agreed that, in response to inquiries, both sides would simply respond "no comment." That leaves it to you, the reader, to creatively guess what may have resolved this dispute.

This was a historic case, attracting national and international attention, especially in Korea. The legal fight had finally come to an end.

Interestingly, on November 5, 2021, the *Montgomery Advertiser* ran a front-page feature story entitled "JOBS OPEN AT PLANT." The subhead was "Hyundai struggles to fill open assembly line jobs in Montgomery." The text of the article went on to read: "When Hyundai opened its Montgomery assembly plant two decades ago, there were 25,000 applicants for about 1,600 jobs. Today, the plant has about 150 assembly line jobs open, and there were twice that many jobs open a few months ago."

## RETURN TO HONEYBEES

Meanwhile, Mike Keller returned to his Southern Sweet Bee pastime that began as a hobby in 1982. It became a small part-time business in 2012. However, upon Keller's termination in 2018, it expanded into a full-time, profitable business. His number of bee colonies doubled from 185 at his termination to 450 by the summer of 2022. That included his removal on March 30, 2022, from my and Leslie's 1908 Old Cloverdale home a colony of 70,000 bees that had established in the attic above our den. This was a huge service to us and a boon to Keller. I can also personally attest that his honey is delicious.

I can only wonder how many times more profitable Hyundai could have been had it developed the talented, dedicated, loyal and hardworking super employee Mike Keller. Indeed, had the Korean automaker let him become their chief American executive, Hyundai might well have challenged Ford Motor and General Motors for the top car manufacturer spot in the world. Sounds like an exaggeration, but that is how multi-talented this blue-collar genius was.

# 9

# Prosecutors Can Be Bullies, Too!

I know what it's like to be a prosecutor. After four years on Wall Street, I began my Alabama legal career in 1975 as an assistant attorney general prosecuting white-collar crime. I have also successfully defended many people of alleged crimes, including three total acquittals of people wrongfully charged with capital murder. There is no way for the defendants to ever be adequately compensated for sitting in jail, without bond, for 18–22 months, while awaiting trial for a murder you didn't commit. Even after vindication at trial, it is hard to collect anything against misguided prosecutors because of sovereign or prosecutorial immunity. Just ask Arthurene Ringstaff, Dennis Heard, and Richard Lee Steele, all clients of mine from the 1980s and '90s, all acquitted of all charges in three different murder trials.

There is little worse than the overwhelming, consuming depression that can hit people charged with a crime for which they are innocent, while contemplating years in prison for something they didn't do. It is a "dark night of the soul," to put it mildly. It happens to far too many people.

As much as I have taken on police brutality, and excessive force, over the years, I have also defended many officers wrongfully charged. In the years 2018–2021, that included the three Selma police officers who were indicted and pursued in one of the worst farces of wrongful prosecution I have ever seen (see Chapter 10).

Don't get me wrong. True crime should be prosecuted vigorously. Innocent victims need to be protected. Good law enforcement is much needed and highly valued. There is also the problem that many jurors do not understand "the presumption of innocence" standard, instinctively believing just the opposite. They also do not understand that the burden of proof is with the prosecution "to prove guilt beyond a reasonable doubt," a very high standard. These misunderstandings make for many wrongful convictions.

The three Selma police officers, long-time veterans Jeff Hardy, Kendall Thomas, and Tori Neeley—two sergeants and a lieutenant—were wrongfully indicted in October 2018. Co-counsel David Sawyer and I filed multiple motions and initially got the first indictment dismissed in May 2019 by Selma Judge Collins Pettway, due to prosecutorial grand jury misconduct. Two weeks later, in June, however, the crazy attorney general's office sent investigator Susan Smith back to Selma to secure a second indictment.

The case stretched out over another two years, while the attorney general's office forced two different African American judges off the case. First, Judge Pettway was removed by the Alabama Court of Criminal Appeals. Months later, the subsequent jurist, Judge Marvin Wiggins, was so vigorously challenged, criticized, and insulted by the Alabama attorney general's office that he voluntarily recused himself. After further delays, a retired white judge, John Bush, was finally assigned to the case, almost three years after the original indictments. Read chapter 10 to find out more about what happened in this enormous travesty of justice.

### U.s. Justice Department Targets Alabama Correctional Officers

Starting in 2019, with a misguided messianic impulse to improve Alabama's prisons, the U.S. Justice Department indicted Alabama correctional officers statewide over issues related to inmate abuse. Though well-intentioned, this effort was terribly counter-productive, making matters worse for inmates. The end result was less correctional officers available for the prisons. That substantially reduced safety for inmates and officers alike.

In my book, *Only in Alabama*, chapter 6 is entitled "Alabama Prisons a Nightmare." There is a discussion of separate cases of four correctional officers wrongfully charged with crimes related to inmate abuse. The four, Cornelius Simpson, Myron Chappell, Jeremy Hester, and Derrick Kelly, had to dig deep into their personal financial pockets to defend themselves against bogus criminal charges. Our firm gave each officer a first-class defense for a reasonable fee and won all four cases.

With hard work, all of these charges were either acquitted, or thrown out in court, no-billed by a grand jury, or dismissed at the last moment by a district attorney of Elmore County, after a jury was impaneled.

## STATE DISTRICT ATTORNEYS MORE REASONABLE

Working with state district attorneys in criminal cases has been a much more pleasant experience than working with Justice Department attorneys out of Washington, D.C. In fact, Daryl Bailey, the Montgomery County D.A., and Randall Houston, the Elmore County D.A., are both highly professional, cordial, and reasonable, even when our interests have been quite contrary. Further, Jefferson County district attorney Danny Carr has won a national award for showing compassion, redemption, and restoration into correctional environments.

## JUSTICE DEPARTMENT ATTORNEYS FROM WASHINGTON, D.C.

The same cannot be said for attorneys outside of the Justice Department in Washington. An exception is David Reese, a fairly pleasant prosecutor with whom to work. One other attorney always talked so fast in trying to convince me about potential conflicts, or about why my client should plead guilty to a lesser offense and get only five years, that I found it hard to get a word in edgewise.

The four correctional officers the Justice Department was picking on in new cases were Willie Burks, Jordan Thomas, Devlon Williams, and Lorenzo Mills Jr. My law partner Joe Guillot worked with me on all four. In the first three cases we had multiple meetings with the Feds. My clients and I were "all ears" listening to what the government lawyers had to say. Fast-talking was their mode, as the Justice Department attorneys tried to talk my clients into entering a guilty plea, which would gain for themselves a lighter sentence (only five years, as opposed to ten, if convicted after trial).

This was not an exciting enticement, and the modus operandi of the Feds was clear. It was to scare, intimidate or induce my clients. One famous federal judge has called this practice "legalized extortion" or "legalized bribery." If the correctional officer tells the federal government something bad about other correctional officers, then his punishment will be lighter, or his situation better, and he can avoid trial. Such an inducement may be accompanied by a shrug, smile, or nod, but later reduced to a plea agreement, heavily worded in favor of the prosecution, with a juicy award for the one pleading guilty. Not a very exciting development for a party defendant, but when compared to a worse outcome for not cooperating, many correctional officers cave in. They then wrongfully spend years in prison.

## WILLIE BURKS

Take Lieutenant Willie Burks for instance. All he was accused of doing was "failing to intervene" in an altercation between Sergeant Oliver and two inmates. Burks did intervene or attempted to. He told the sergeant to stop, and afterwards, the said officer did stop. In fact, Oliver wrote down in a report that Burks told him to stop, and Oliver admitted this to a grand jury. What Burks didn't do, the essence of the indictment against him, is "jump in like Superman" to break up the altercation the moment he first saw it, as portrayed in a video. Unfortunately, for Burks, on a scale of one to ten, he was suffering a nine in severe back pain at the time, for which he received surgery only a few months later.

The Justice Department's pressure for Burks to plead was a misguided and bullying tactic freely employed on state correctional officers to get them to suddenly remember something bad about Burks. Unfortunately, this widely used tactic is deemed proper by the Feds, against DOC officers, getting them to capitulate against their fellow officers. Burks had three other eyewitness officers who gained advantage for themselves in sentencing by testifying against him.

After many continuances, the Burks case finally came to court on June 21–23 before the Honorable Myron Thompson, whom I admire. I disagreed with this great judge's allowing a lead prosecutor Katherine DeVor to strike so many jury panelists "for cause," simply because she and the court deemed them too pro-law enforcement. That included the courthouse security guard, a former Montgomery police officer. I kept protesting that she (the prosecutor) was also on the "law enforcement" side. That was because, after all, "the Feds were the ones prosecuting." DeVor, as was her right, was searching for jurors unsympathetic to Burks. Since Burks himself was "a law enforcement officer," DeVor wanted jurors unsympathetic to law enforcement.

Consequently, we ended up with a jury sympathetic to the inmate. Hurting Burks the most was the Fed's constant playing of a video, even in opening arguments, showing Burks's subordinate, Sergeant Ulysses Oliver, striking two inmates, while Burks appeared to be standing by, doing little to interfere. It was very damaging that two other officers under Burks turned on him, with incentivized plea agreements to testify against him.

Suddenly these officers changed their earlier stories, and for the first time the officers say never heard Burks tell Oliver to stop. Late in the weeks before trial, the pleaders suddenly remembered hearing Burks say what happened to the inmates was "fair." Oliver also caved into a plea agreement, suddenly saying he wasn't sure Burks ever told him to stop. That totally contradicted Oliver's earlier signed, written statement.

Several people present in the courtroom told me my closing argument was one of the best they ever heard. The jury came back with a conviction against Burks for "failure to intervene" against Sgt. Oliver's, because he was striking inmates. On February 4, 2022, Willie Burks was sentenced to 108 months in prison, or nine years. This was draconian in my view and made Burks a scapegoat for a bigger problem, for which Burks was unfairly blamed.

To contend that Burks was bullied may appear an ironic overstatement. That was because of the jury's finding that Burks didn't do enough to stop a subordinate sergeant from bullying an inmate. The difference is that the prosecution had the incredible advantage plea agreements to give to witnesses. This provided the correctional officers incentive to modify their stories, overwhelming Burks in a form of legalized bribery. That advantage has an underlying smell of "bullyism."

## AFTERMATH OF SENTENCING

Unlike our state court system, once sentenced by the federal courts, it is rare for a defendant to remain out of prison while pursuing an appeal, on bond or otherwise. Former governor Don Siegelman and business magnate Richard Scrushy were both immediately locked up after conviction and subjected to a brutal immediate journey to prison.

By contrast, Willie Burks, though convicted on June 23, was allowed out of jail without bond until the sentencing date of February 4, 2022. Even more unexpectedly, Judge Thompson allowed Burks until mid-March to turn himself in to prison.

A few days later co-counsel Joe Guillot and I met with Burks and his brother to discuss grounds for appeal and the business arrangements for the same. Burks was eager to pursue the appeal, despite the cost. Despite its rarity, I prepared a Rule 18 USC §3143 motion for Burks to remain on release pending appeal to the Eleventh Circuit U.S. Court of Appeals.

For such a motion to be granted the lower court (in our case, Judge Thompson) must determine there is a "substantial question on appeal likely to result in reversal on new trial." Believing Judge Thompson to be a near-perfectionist in his rulings, we didn't expect him or any other judge to grant such a motion.

But he did. Thank you, Judge. In a five-page order dated March 2, 2022, Judge Thompson stated:

> Burks asserts several grounds for appeal at this time. Among these, he challenges the court's decision to strike a juror as biased and has preserved this issue for appeal. He also challenges the court's guidelines determinations during sentencing, including its determination to increase the base offense level because the underlying offense was committed using a dangerous weapon, because it resulted in bodily injury, because the victim was restrained, and because defendant Burks obstructed or impeded justice. The court is of the opinion that, while the matter posed is quite close, one or more of these issues present a substantial question of law that, if resolved in Burks's favor, may be likely to result in a term of imprisonment less than the expected duration of the appeal process.
>
> Accordingly, it is ORDERED that defendant Willie M. Burks III's motion for release pending appeal to the Eleventh Circuit (Doc. 214) is granted.

My paralegal Cesaire McPherson let go a whoop of celebration in bringing me the order. So, I called both Burks and Guillot. The former was almost in tears, with my law partner Joe yelling his delight: "Now I can have Willie's help" on the appeal.

The three of us had our work cut out for us.

## JORDAN THOMAS

The Jordan Thomas case arose out of a Bibb Correctional Facility south of Tuscaloosa, with a trial in Tuscaloosa scheduled for the week of May 3–7, 2021. Thomas, originally born in Eastern Europe, as a baby was adopted by missionaries. He was barely a month past 19 when accused of kicking and hitting an inmate on September 13, 2021. Two other older correctional officers, Keith Finch, and Kevin Blaylock, like Thomas, felt they had done nothing wrong. But all three were indicted for violating the U.S. Constitutional right of the inmate to be free of cruel and unusual punishment forbidden by the Eighth Amendment. The trial exposed the Bibb prison as a jungle besieged by knives, blades, other weapons, and drugs. It was also grossly understaffed by 12–15 correctional officers watching out for 1,800 inmates, crammed into five adjoining dormitories.

The Feds claimed that Thomas, Finch and Blaylock, in containing escaping inmate Danny Little, were too rough, and used unnecessary force.

My client Thomas was just four months out of the training academy, still on probation, when on September 12, 2018, an incident got him into big trouble. Inmate Little was indisputably high on drugs when he broke out of Dorm A that evening, bolting for the front door, where he encountered Thomas. Little knocked Thomas on his back. Jumping up, Thomas grabbed a baton and rapped the inmate on the legs. He struck him once with an open hand. Thomas also used his leg, in a sweeping maneuver, to knock the inmate off of his feet. Two other officers acted similarly, and all three were charged with cruel and unusual punishment, in violation of the Eighth Amendment to the U.S. Constitution.

"Code Red" was screamed by both Thomas and the female officer guarding the dorm exit. That term means that an "officer's life is in danger." The other two officers, Keith Finch and Kevin Blaylock came running at top speed over, to assist Thomas. It took all three officers to finally hand-cuff and contain inmate Little.

Video covered it all, and that resulted in the Justice Department engaging in great "Monday morning quarterbacking." This was despite evidence showing that Bibb prison was a dangerous jungle continuously threatening the lives and health of inmates and officers alike.

At a first trial started on Monday, May 3, the jury retired after only three days of trial and was out all day deliberating. By Friday, May 7, the jury announced it was "hopelessly deadlocked on all three officers" and couldn't reach the required unanimous verdict. Judge Scott Coogler declared a hung jury and a mistrial. This was a victory of sorts, denying a conviction to federal prosecutors who enjoy a 97 percent conviction rate nationally. Judge Coogler scheduled a retrial on November 1, 2021. In May 2021, due to differences in strategy with a strong-willed client, I withdrew from further representation of Thomas. I felt it best for him to take the stand, but he didn't want to.

A retrial occurred on November 1–3, 2021. With new Birmingham counsel leading him, Thomas caved in, accepted a plea for a lesser time in prison, and agreed to testify against the other two, and so he did. That strategy backfired when the other two were acquitted after a full trial and excellent representation by two brilliant Birmingham attorneys, Richard Jaffe and Emory Anthony.

## Devlon Williams

Devlon Williams, like Burks and Thomas, was a client of mine for over a year before he was indicted in March 2021. My law partner Joe Guillot and I were due to defend him in January 2022. Williams's defense is that he was protecting himself against a knife attack by an inmate.

Actually, knife attacks in jails and prisons are omnipresent and exceedingly real. Most inmates will confirm that all fellow inmates carry knives or other sharp objects to defend themselves. These weapons have obvious offensive capabilities, to stab or bludgeon someone else, which is frequently done to fellow inmates and sometimes to correctional officers.

The trial finally began on Monday, May 9, 2022, before Judge Austin

Huffaker of the Middle District of Alabama. This was four years and two months after the alleged crime on March 8, 2012, namely subjecting an inmate to cruel and unusual punishment. Also thrown in were counts of falsification of records and obstruction of justice.

With the assistance of law partner Joe Guillot and paralegal Wendy Newman, I was psyched up the day the trial began. We picked 14 jurors, eight black and six white. I felt good about the number of African American jurors, since Williams was black and the alleged victim, David Harmon, was white. We tried to strike the worst prospective jurors. We felt females were probably worse for us than males, given three female nurse witnesses against us.

Williams had a big family prayer team covering him, and I was a part of that. The prosecution consisted of two very able federal prosecutors, David Reese of Washington, D.C., and Eric Cook, formerly of Tennessee but relocated to Montgomery.

One of our defenses was that the Alabama Department of Corrections had already fully investigated the matter and found only minor discipline of a three-day suspension appropriate. That kept Williams on his job at Staton Correctional Center.

Another defense was that it was actually another correctional officer, Joseph Manigan, who had done the damage via kicking Harmon in the ribs. Manigan turned state's evidence, accepting a legalized bribe to testify against Williams in return for a substantially reduced sentence. At trial, in response to questions from the prosecutor, Manigan admitted that he had lied at least 15 times in various reports.

We subpoenaed several other Staton correctional officers who testified in Williams's defense. That included a female guard in the tower, she denied the prosecution's allegations that Williams banged the inmate into an opening gate. Another correctional officer testified that he had seen the allegedly badly wounded inmate doing calisthenics, including push-ups and sit-ups the day after his injuries. That proved the inmate's con artistry in the original suicide attempt. We also poked holes in cross-examining many of the government's witnesses.

After the three-day trial and full day of deliberations, the jury reported for the third time it was "hopelessly deadlocked." Judge Huffaker gave a dynamite charge, but it did not work. After all, trying to get 14 very diverse jurors to agree on anything is difficult. We had 14 jurors, but none were alternates. A "hung jury" is considered a victory for the defense. It is not the 100 percent victory of acquittal. The trial was rescheduled for November 14, 2022 (one day after my 76th birthday). It was my hope to convince the Feds to exercise prosecutorial discretion in not pursuing the case again, especially after we learned from the federal defender's office about the 12–2 in our favor. Despite multiple letters to lead prosecutor David Reese, to Rose Gipson, head of the Civil Rights Division, and even to U.S. Attorney General Merrick Garland, the prosecution insisted on trying it again.

## LORENZO MILLS

Lorenzo Mills was the last of the four coming to see me in November 2020. At that time, he had only state charges. When it happened, he was at a different prison than Devlon Williams, and knew nothing about Williams's case. Yet, the Feds, seemingly afraid of having my partner Joe Guillot and me defending Mills in that case, suggested there might be a conflict in our representing both Mills and Williams. Baloney, I said. This reflects the Justice Department's unfairness. Meanwhile, Mills insisted he wanted no one else as his attorney but me. Mills personally left our firm in near tears over the possibility of our being conflicted out. "Near tears" is touching when you see it coming from a mature man weighing 350 pounds and standing 5'10". Obviously, big people can cry, and the Feds know how to cause it.

Later, for financial reasons only, Mills and I decided that his federal criminal defense would best be provided by a seasoned federal public defender at no cost to him. I continued to represent Mills in the Elmore County Circuit Court on parallel state charges.

## 10

# Selma Police Bully Attorney General

In Chapter 24 of *Only in Alabama*, entitled "Opening Up the Flood-gates," I describe what a hypocrite Alabama Attorney General Steve Marshall is for his 180-degree reversal on Alabama's Anti PAC-to-PAC transfer law.

Under that law, it is illegal for a political candidate to take financial contributions from PACs (Political Action Committees) whose source of money comes from another PAC, thus hiding the identities of the underlying donors—ranging from the Mafia to opioid manufacturers. Marshall strongly supported this law when he defended an appeal to the U.S. Supreme Court seeking to overturn it. Yet, less than two years later, to help his 2018 race for the office of attorney general, Steve Marshall took $750,000 from a Republican PAC, with no disclosure of its original donors. This is how the PAC-to-PAC political universe covers up dirty money. This is how Marshall opened the floodgates in Alabama to make political contributions from nefarious sources. Shame on him!

Marshall also pursued three of Selma's finest police officers, all African Americans, when the attorney general's office caused them to be indicted for allegedly lying to his office and/or giving false information to his investigators. City of Selma officers Jeff Hardy, Kendall Thomas, and Toriano Neely were all frivolously charged with misrepresenting the condition of the Selma Police Department evidence room. All these officers did was commit the grievous sin of saying that the evidence room was not neat and orderly enough while the state investigators said, "Oh no, it was a mess." My clients were indicted over what basically amounted to a difference of opinion. In addition, they were stripped of their jobs and dignity and left financially destitute. Their good names, reputations, and integrities were tarnished and sullied. This was a dark, cold night for the soul of each. This was also bullying of the worst sort by an abusive public official, namely Alabama's attorney general.

Thank goodness for the brilliant lawyer David Sawyer, initially of-counsel to the McPhillips Shinbaum firm. He assisted me on this case. We filed a bevy of motions in 2018–2019, mostly crafted by David, leading to Dallas County Circuit Judge Collins Pettway ruling in favor of all three police officers. Pettway in fact dismissed the case, due to grand jury misconduct in May 2019 by state investigator Susan Smith.

We held a press conference and enjoyed the moment of victory that was ballyhooed in Alabama on TV, radio, and newspaper. A framed copy of the *Montgomery Advertiser* picture of the three officers, David Sawyer, and me hangs above a sofa in our firm's main-floor "Hall of Fame."

Amazingly, the same Susan Smith darted back over from Montgomery to Selma. She succeeded in getting the three officers reindicted for the exact same offense. That led to another two years and three months of legal work before we finally got all the charges dismissed.

This bullying prosecution by Marshall's office was coated with a deep-seated racism, in my opinion. Immediately upon the second indictment, the AG's Office put great effort into having Judge Pettway, himself an African American, removed from the case. This was after Judge Pettway refused their request to do so voluntarily. Lead Assistant Attorney General Andrew Arrington cited nebulous reasons for filing a mandamus appeal to the Alabama Court of Criminal Appeals, which effectively hijacked the case for almost another year, 2019–2020. This pushed the case well into the pandemic . . . Surprise! The conservative Alabama Supreme Court of nine Republicans granted Arrington's petition to remove Judge Pettway.

At that point, we were well into the summer of 2020. The attorney general's office then sought to remove the next judge, newly appointed Marvin Wiggins, another African American. There was no good reason to do so, except the AG's office was in fear of losing. The fact was that Wiggins was Black. The blatant racism was obvious and stunk to high heaven! In a Zoom conference in August 2020, the attorney general's office unfairly attacked Wiggins to his face. They criticized a ruling of the judge from 15 years earlier. Not enjoying the controversy, Judge Wiggins recused himself.

That left us in late 2020 with retired Elmore County Circuit Judge John Bush, a Caucasian appointed by the Administrative Office of Courts. I had known Bush from his earlier career work as a neighboring lawyer in private practice, and later as a judge in Wetumpka. I therefore believed he would be fair, and we didn't contest his appointment. And he was fair!

Sawyer and I filed multiple other motions after several other telephone hearings. That was when the attorney general's office recognized how bad a case it had, one they ultimately could lose. Accordingly, newly appointed Assistant Attorney General Riggs Walker honorably deemed it wise to back off. He must have convinced Marshall to avoid an embarrassing defeat.

Accordingly, on Friday, August 13, with a five-day trial looming on August 23–27 in Dallas County, Sawyer and I were shocked to hear that Attorney General Marshall had decided to completely surrender. No one from their office had called us in advance to advise they were filing a motion to dismiss all charges against all three officers. Judge Bush wasted no time in dismissing the case with prejudice the next day.

Thus concluded a long, hard arduous journey for officers Hardy, Thomas, and Neely. This was not unlike the Israelites in the Wilderness, who appeared to be over, at least as far as their criminal jeopardies were concerned. On Friday, August 16 we released to the media an announcement regarding the outcome. This time, at my clients' request, no news conference was called. We did say that the officers would continue their civil suit against the City of Selma, its former Mayor Dario Melton, and former Selma Parks and Recreation Department Director Sean VanDiver for lost wages and mental anguish.

That suit was originally filed in 2019 for damages against the bullying City of Selma and its top officials for putting the officers on leave without pay. This was after being indicted, but not convicted. This suit was stayed later in 2019, but it was reactivated in 2021 after the criminal charges were dismissed. Our clients had also contemplated a separate suit for damages against the investigator who wrongfully caused the situation. Thus, a malicious prosecution cause of action could have accrued at the date of dismissal of the criminal charges. Sawyer and I suggested the officers might use other counsel for such a case.

# 11

# Ronita Wade Vanquishes Bully Mayor

What goes around comes around. Selma Mayor Dario Melton learned it the hard way.

Talk about taking on bullies! Selma city treasurer Ronita Wade had no idea what pain and anguish she was about to suffer at the hands of politician Dario Melton upon his August 2016 election as mayor of historic Selma. Ronita had to beat this bully mayor four times legally before she finally tamed him—twice before the Selma City Council and twice in Court.

Ronita's good friends, Terry and Gerald Chestnut, a brother and sister duo, campaigned hard in 2016 to elect Melton, delivering to him the valuable political mantle of their famous father, the late and renowPned civil rights leader, J. L. Chestnut Jr. It apparently made a significant difference in the outcome of the election. Dario Melton, then a 37-year-old state representative, defeated two more-prominent, more-senior opponents, the incumbent Mayor George Evans and former two-term Mayor James Perkins.

Less than a year after Melton assumed the mayorship in November 2016, he politically ambushed Wade. This repeated itself not once, not twice, but thrice. The young mayor, narcissistically flexing his political muscle, first fired Wade as treasurer in September 2017. He did it a second time in December 2017, and a third time in September 2018. The Selma City Council reinstated Wade the first two times shortly thereafter. The third time it required an order from the Dallas County Circuit Court, in May 2018, to reinstate her.

I represented Wade in all three reinstatements, but it became obvious that we needed to take this to a higher level. So in 2019, newly associated lawyer David Sawyer and I filed a new lawsuit for Ronita Wade, this time in federal court, headquartered in Mobile, but with Selma as its northwest division. We alleged a violation of the U.S. Constitution's First Amendment freedom of political association guarantee. Shortly afterwards, on behalf of a former Selma parks and recreation assistant director, we filed a second federal lawsuit alleging sex discrimination, sexual harassment, and illegal retaliation—shades of Wade. The two cases, both filed in Mobile, took parallel paths, with the same defense attorney, the energetic Rick Howard of Montgomery, representing Selma in both cases.

Wade's and the former parks and recreation assistant director's legal missiles survived summary judgment attacks in the U.S. District Court from Dario Melton's defense team. Sawyer and I made two round trips of 360 miles to Mobile, defending against these motions. Had either been granted, it would have knocked us completely out of court. We survived, vanquishing the substantial evidence standard to continue the cases. According to knowledgeable U.S. Magistrate Judge Steven Doyle of Montgomery, 60 percent of such motions, at least in the federal district court in Montgomery, succeed for defendants, and Mobile is thought to be more conservative or pro-business than Montgomery. This leads to far too many decent plaintiff's cases being dismissed, due to ridiculously high standards of proof holdings.

Not long afterwards we also filed suit for another Selma client, former fire chief Tony Stephens, but in the Dallas County Circuit Court. Law partner Kenneth Shinbaum helped me represent Stephens, while Sawyer continually provided leadership assistance on both the recreation assistant director's and Wade's cases, both fraught with multiple issues.

Getting to trial can sometimes take several years, and during the Coronavirus era, we got pushed back even further. Finally, in the fall of 2021 we got to bat in Wade's case in a run-down Selma federal courthouse that had not been used for trials for three years even before the pandemic began. The air-conditioning wasn't working the first day of trial, September 27, 2021, giving the courthouse a feel of the 1950s era. Old-fashioned fans were noisily whirring. Everyone strained to hear, as we were required to wear masks, muffling our voices. Three cheers for the coronavirus era!

Fortunately, in Wade's case, a pleasant, and professional Judge Kristi

Dubose of Mobile presided. All the attorneys had double vaccinations and were required to speak from a distance. Judge Dubose made us speak directly into the microphone, as best we could. Fortunately, my "see-through" mask allowed the jury to see my smile. It also gave me more space for speaking and breathing. The cloth masks worn by others covered 60 percent of their faces and muffled their voices. The pandemic was wreaking its due. Thus, during the September 27–29, 2021, trial we battled, face masks intact, like gladiators.

This was my third federal jury trial in 2021 in five months—in Tuscaloosa in May 2021, in Montgomery in June 2021, and in Selma in September 2021. Even in the early fall of 2021, Montgomery County Chief Circuit Judge Johnny Hardwick, still fearing the pandemic, had not yet allowed jury trials in my home county.

The Ronita Wade–Dario Melton trial was a classic. It began on Monday, September 27 with picking a jury and giving opening arguments. Originally witnesses were not supposed to be present until the second day of this epic battle between Selma's former titans. But everything began so quickly under Judge Kristi Dubose that she instructed me to call our first witness by no later than mid-afternoon Monday.

I got on the phone and hustled up witnesses previously advised not to come until Tuesday. I quickly reached the brother and sister Chestnuts. Like their famous father J. L. Chestnut Jr., they exuded an effective courtroom presence, especially daughter Gerald. She was our star witness and testified how Dario told her on Day 2 of her new job in February 2017 that "Ronita will be the first I will get rid of as mayor, and then the rest," referring to other supporters of outgoing Mayor George Evans.

In saying this, Melton may not have realized he was violating the First Amendment of the U.S. Constitution's "freedom of political association." Of our four original causes of action in the lawsuit, this was the sole one Judge Dubose allowed us to take to the jury. She trimmed away three others (including procedural due process) in earlier summary judgment rulings from Mobile.

A female friend of Wade's from Atlanta, testifying at trial, confirmed Melton's political purpose at the Golden Ranch Restaurant in Selma in

July 2016. There Melton approached Wade and her friend, seeking Wade's valuable support. But Wade, as politely as she knew how, rejected the request, citing her allegiance to then Selma Mayor George Evans.

Our next witness, Tameka Sikes, walked across the street from the Dallas County district attorney's office, to confirm Melton's pattern and practice. She testified that Melton solicited her twice in a church where he ministered, and even threatened her that, if she didn't support him, she too would lose her job, when he became the new mayor of Selma. He should have known better!

Former Selma fire chief Tony Stephens testified that during a meeting of cabinet-level officials, Melton demanded that the others present "find out anything they could against Ronita Wade, and if necessary, make something up." The next witness, a former Selma Parks and Recreation official, chimed in with similar comments about her bad experiences with Melton. He had also approached this official, but, after being rebuffed later sought to rid himself of her as well.

Ronita Wade testified superbly from the stand herself, unfolding her sad story of three terminations and the substantial interference by Mayor Melton with her job.

Melton's first witness, former chief of staff Ollie Davidson, ended up helping us more than helping Melton, admitting that he (Davidson) had apologized to Wade on the job about the way Melton was treating her. The mayor's second witness, Jared Cunningham, who temporarily replaced Wade as treasurer, also helped us considerably, though surely not intending to, as he confirmed the nitpicking nature of Melton's complaints about Wade.

Melton's own testimony came across as evasive, argumentative, and lacking in credibility, as he insincerely attempted to explain away his terrible treatment of Wade. Melton was especially weak in not being able to explain how his oft-expressed excuse for terminating Wade, namely that she was "under investigation," was not his real reason for removing her. That "pretext" was nothing but an investigation initiated by himself. We called it a "sham investigation," a term the press and others in Selma were quick to jump on and repeat.

Not surprisingly, able defense attorney Rick Howard was not a happy camper with how his witnesses were testifying and decided to call no more.

Closing arguments began Wednesday morning with Sawyer taking 10 minutes; I took the remaining 20 minutes. We urged the jury to send a message with a strong verdict against Melton, finding that he violated the First Amendment "freedom of political association" guarantee.

That is exactly what the jury did, returning a $50,000 verdict to Wade. When added to an additional $150,000 in attorney fees, the total court verdict was worth $200,000. Not bad; not a record, but not bad.

Accordingly, the jury sent a message, as I had asked it to do, not only to Melton but to mayors of other towns and cities around Alabama, and maybe to mayors outside the state.

Wade herself was elated. The heavy weight and burden she had carried so long was alleviated, or at least significantly subdued. To me she looked like a new person . . . or like a boxer who scored a knockout.

So justice still does occur in America, but it took a "lady of courage and endurance," a hero or heroine like Ronita Wade, to stand up to and pop back a bully mayor.

## 12

# Institutional Racism Confronted

Yes, so much of racism in America is institutional, and it is bullying whether in the private or public sector. It was my honor in 2019–2021 to represent two sets of African American women with the courage and tenacity to challenge institutional racism in both sectors.

## ZELMA SMITH AND SAVANNAH MAYES VERSUS ELMORE COUNTY BOARD OF EDUCATION

One set included two ladies, Zelma Smith and Savannah Mayes, both cafeteria workers at the Coosada Elementary School. They took on the Elmore County Board of Education for repeatedly passing over them in promotions given to clearly less qualified and less experienced Caucasian coworkers. Smith, the mother of Coosada police chief Leon Smith, raised her son to stand up to injustice, and she could do no less herself.

Likewise, Mayes encountered the same experience at Coosada Elementary. No one called her or Smith any racist names. The discrimination was more endemic, less overt, but in the system. Blacks were supposed to know their place at the lower end of the totem pole, and the whites knew their upper status . . . supposedly . . . at least until two courageous ladies challenged it.

Smith at 55 and Mayes at 47, both well into middle age, had had enough. They were tired of being given excuses such as "you ate on the job," while their white counterparts did the same things and got away with it.

Therefore, I filed charges with the Equal Employment Opportunity Commission (EEOC), first for Smith on November 5, 2019, and then for Mayes on January 20, 2020.

As long as the EEOC can receive any information from the "Responding

Employer" that the employer was "not discriminating," then it will almost always come up with a "neutral" finding, while still issuing a right-to-sue letter to the complaining parties. This it did for both ladies.

Smith and Mayes knew they were wronged and wronged in similar ways. Upon my recommendation, they combined their resources to file a joint suit and shared in the attorney and filing fees.

My office manager and paralegal Amy Strickland played a big role at both the front end and the back end, with soothing and persuasive words, helping to resolve the Smith and Mayes cases. In the end both ladies felt vindicated by the outcome after case-ending negotiations with confidentiality clauses. They also felt justified that their legal action would make "the powers that be" at the Elmore County Board of Education be more sensitive generally to the needs of African American employees.

## ARNISHA JOHNSON AND STEPHANIE MOORER VERSUS MANPOWER

Meanwhile, near the same time on November 12, 2019, two younger African American women, Arnisha Johnson and Stephanie Moorer, lost their jobs at Manpower's office in Greenville, Alabama, jobs they had held for seven years (Johnson) and nine years (Moorer).

Manpower was essentially a "temp agency," and both Johnson and Moorer were recruiters of prospective employees for job openings and/or "job needs" that Manpower would be contacted about.

A majority of the applicants needing jobs were African Americans, and one would think that made Johnson and Moorer all the more desirable for Manpower's top brass. Unfortunately, upper management didn't see it that way, as a newer and more aggressive Caucasian woman bounced in, and, with Manpower's acquiescence, the best job openings started going to her. My two clients were bright, personable, and mature but suffered the disadvantage of being "born Black." Simple as that, in my opinion. Neither client had done anything wrong.

An atmosphere of racial tension had grown in the Manpower office when repeatedly condescending Caucasian comments kept putting Black employees down. One frequent term was the "little brown boy" reference to people of mixed racial heritage. Even the oft-used "Black people" was a more subtly derogatory reference. Not-so-subtle digs included, "How can *these people* afford $200 shoes, when most are on welfare?" Not a flattering a racial stereotype.

The worst part was that the best opportunities for placing applicants started going to a newly hired white female, Amanda, and she was the one uttering many of these racial comments.

Then all of a sudden, on November 1, 2019, both Arnisha and Stephanie were fired by Manpower. Ouch! They wasted no time coming to see me. On November 12, 2019, I filed race discrimination charges for both with the EEOC.

During January and February 2020, with the help of renowned EEOC mediator Jonathan Jones and working with a female St. Louis attorney representing Manpower, we almost negotiated a very good settlement for both my clients. But then Covid burst upon everyone like a big sucker punch. Suddenly Manpower declared all negotiations off. This also happened in several of my other cases.

That left us with no choice but to file a suit. Once again, a combined lawsuit, with Johnson and Moorer as co-plaintiffs, was filed.

Covid hit hard from mid-March 2020 until well into 2021, causing the wheels of justice to turn slowly on many cases, including these two. At times, few people were out on the streets, but our office never closed for a single day of the pandemic. And clients kept coming!

I associated attorney Tanika Finney, of counsel to our law firm, to assist me in the discovery phase of our two clients' cases against Manpower. That included three depositions she took of the opposing side's witnesses, as well as defending Johnson and Moorer in depositions taken of them by Manpower. I think Finney did a good job. There were the usual ton of documents, a veritable mishmash, to plow through.

Unfortunately, the judge assigned to this case (I will not name her) had a strong "status quo" philosophy. Based on her rulings in another similar case, I felt a defense summary judgment motion might well threaten our outcome.

As a matter of legal ethics, it is improper to talk about what was said in a mediation or what resulted from one, and I won't do so here. Nonetheless,

U.S. Magistrate Judge Stephen Doyle helped us address certain issues to clarify our positions. One such weakness was the higher-up manager in Tennessee (a male) who made the decision to terminate my clients. The opposition insisted he was the decision-maker and knew nothing about the racial disparities and insults issued in its Greenville, Alabama, office. That man was simply responding to certain mathematical facts, they insisted, making it hard to pin race discrimination on him. We argued in response that this higher manager was influenced by recommendations from lower-level women who endured actual racial bias.

In the second week of October 2021, we "resolved" both the Johnson–Moorer case versus Manpower and the Smith–Mayes complaints versus the Elmore County Board of Education.

To make it happen, we reduced our attorney fees substantially and helped craft multi-faceted relief. In both sets of cases, we had satisfied clients in the end. To me, that is more important than getting a big fee.

Obviously, the corporate defendant would tell this story differently, but in both cases we believe the forces of institutional racial discrimination were confronted and stymied, if nothing more. This type of bully should be more careful the next time around, at least at Manpower and the Elmore County Board of Education. This was two, or maybe four, small steps for justice! All were marching in the right direction.

# Mental Health Industry Can Also Bully

Mental health centers are designed to help people deal with or treat mental health problems. Right? Wrong, if you were an older African American employee working for the Cahaba Mental Health Center in Selma in late 2019 or early 2020.

Just ask Elizabeth Smith, a 62-year-old Black female therapist who loyally gave her heart and soul for the mental health cause for 31 years of her life, helping thousands of clients before she was unceremoniously bullied into retirement on December 2, 2019. And was dumped for something she didn't do! As stated two days later in the public record charge of wrongful race and age discrimination filed with the Equal Employment Opportunity Commission (EEOC) in Birmingham, Smith said:

> I was astonished and greatly disappointed to hear not only of my termination, but the pretextual reason for it, namely that I had "fraudulently" constructed an inaccurate consultant's request via an interoffice document that never went to the client in question.
>
> . . . I genuinely believed I was doing a favor for a subordinate therapist, namely Ms. Bethie Hill (fictitious name substituted). Further, I "had nothing to gain personally" and actually gained nothing from my preparing the document in question. Additionally, I caused no harm to anyone in the document preparation. Moreover, I sent the document in advance to Ms. Bethie Hill, for her review, which provided ample opportunity for Ms. Hill to object and request a correction, had she wanted to."

But Hill, a decent and competent young Caucasian employee, did not do so. It wasn't until a contract psychiatrist, namely Dr. Patrice Donahue, raised a stink that suddenly Hill proclaimed that she had never approved of the change in advance. This left Smith appearing devious. Which she wasn't. And for what? She had nothing to gain. She was simply trying to help her subordinate. Smith soon experienced the old lesson that "no good deed ever goes unpunished."

Smith insisted in her EEOC charge:

> My document creation reflected a goodwill intent to provide clarity among all parties involved, and again Ms. Hill never expressed to me any issues or problems with the consult. At the time, again I thought it would be helpful to Ms. Hill as a sister team member, and as her supervisor.

The consultant's request was simply an interoffice document the prospective client never saw, and whose name will not be revealed here due to privacy and HIPAA protection reasons. The document nonetheless became a public record in two different courts, the Dallas County Circuit Court and the U.S. District Court for the Southern District of Alabama. The first was Smith's appeal of an unemployment compensation denial. The second was Smith's lawsuit for race and age discrimination against Cahaba Mental Health.

With the Cahaba client's name redacted, the document read as follows:

> Request for consultation concerning: I was told by Ms. Smith that you recommended that the client get Med. Monitoring at Day Tx. I do recollect him getting it when he was previously in our Day Tx. Program, and I'm sure he was getting it while living at Cahaba Place. Can you clarify your recommendation on this consult. Thanks!

Hardly an ultra-sensitive or super confidential document, and certainly no rip-off of anyone! Although prepared by Smith, my client instead placed the name of Bethie Hill, rather than Smith's name, as the requesting party. Indeed Smith never said the client was Hill's, nor her own (Smith's). In fact, the client belonged only to Cahaba Mental Health. Further, Smith's only personal gain was the satisfaction of helping her junior employee. Smith soon crossed through Hill's name and wrote in her own name,

"Elizabeth Smith," on the Consultant's Request, correcting the problem. Sounds confusing, doesn't it? But it shouldn't have been. It was certainly not fraud, and Cahaba's leadership should have quickly known that.

Although the issue first emerged on September 24, 2019, no one said anything to Smith about it and gave her virtually no chance to explain how innocent, and how helpful, was her intent. Instead, the flabbergasted, Smith was fired two weeks later on October 9, 2019.

Unfortunately, this minute incident gave Cahaba's executive director (name omitted) the excuse she was looking for to get rid of Smith.

At worst, we strongly contended, progressive discipline short of termination should have been used. Given Smith's 31 years of excellent employment at Cahaba, that would have been far more appropriate. Smith never received any warning, reprimand, or even a suspension during her long tenure. Moreover, the Cahaba Personnel and Safety Policy and Procedures Manual set forth ample provisions for progressive discipline and should have applied to Smith, unless there was an ulterior motive by management in getting rid of her.

Meanwhile, the Cahaba Center, trying to save itself a few dollars, even opposed Smith's unemployment compensation when she filed for it on October 13, 2019, four days after her termination. This was "pennywise but pound foolish," to use an old English expression. It ended up costing Cahaba much more. The indignity motivated Elizabeth Smith to come see me, and it motivated my work.

When Smith first came, I didn't realize I would end up representing her in both state and federal court on two different but related issues . . . both the (a) unemployment denial and (b) a federal race and age discrimination claim.

After Smith was finally denied her unemployment "pennies," we first exhausted our appellate remedies within the Board of Appeals of the State Department of Labor, before filing suit against Cahaba Mental Health and the Labor Department on July 1, 2020, in the Dallas County Circuit Court. Of necessity, we also named Alabama Attorney General Steve Marshall. We stated in our Notice of Appeal petition:

The board was incorrect in upholding the findings, conclusion, and decision of the Administrative Hearing Officer that the Claimant (Elizabeth Smith) was discharged from work for a dishonest or criminal act committed in connection with work or for sabotage or an act endangering the safety of others . . . § 25–4-78(3)(a) Code of Alabama, 1975 (see Exhibits A & B).

In paragraphs 4 and 5 of our appeal to the Dallas County Circuit Court, we stated for Smith that:

4. Contrary to the Board's finding, it is undisputed that there was "no previous warning of any type," nor was there any previous action by Claimant remotely resembling what the Claimant was discharged for. (emphasis added)

5. Further the "document" the Claimant is accused of falsifying was a document the Appellant (Ms. Smith) actually showed to the therapist (Ms. Bethie Hill) whose name was on said document, and said therapist had the opportunity to express opposition to the document but never did so. Instead, when Claimant questioned her about it, said therapist (Ms. Hill) said "it was fine."

And then we added the following additional paragraphs:

6. The Claimant, who was actually supervisor of the therapist Ms. Hill in question at the time of the alleged "falsification," was simply trying to "assist the therapist" in better understanding the treatment nuances needed to be received by the patient, all in the patient's best interest. In fact, Claimant Smith had nothing to gain personally, and gained nothing financially or otherwise, from assisting her subordinate therapist. (emphasis added)

7. Therapist Hill changed her initial concurrence with Claimant's supervisory assistance, after a certain psychiatrist doctor objected to the document, and in doing so, therapist Hill benefitted herself personally by changing her story. Indeed, after Claimant's dismissal, Ms. Hill was promoted to take over the supervisor position Claimant previously held. (emphasis added)

The word "pretext" in the legal world means "not the real reason" or a ruse, or cover-up for the real reason. Thus, our unemployment petition hit Cahaba hard on this issue, stating:

> 8. Reflecting on the pretextual nature of the reasons given for Claimant's termination is that said "reasons" were changed three times by the "Employer." (1) During the first time, at the point of her termination, Claimant was accused of "committing fraud." That is all that was mentioned by the Employer. (2) The second time, during a telephone interview with the Unemployment hearing officer, Claimant was then accused of "falsification of documents." (3) Finally, at the Board of Appeals hearing, the Employer for the first time developed a new reason, namely a "dishonest or criminal act, sabotage, or an act endangering the safety of others committed in connection with his work."

We added in bold print that:

> 9. The truth is, however, there was no sabotage, no endangerment to the safety of others, no use of illegal drugs, and no refusal to submit to a blood or urine test, nor was there any previous warning, and there was no evidence to support any of the foregoing. (emphasis added)
>
> 10. There was no sabotage because Ms. Hill knew that, with Ms. Smith's greater knowledge of the patient and longer experience with him, she (Ms. Smith) was better able to address nuances and issues in the report. Indeed, Claimant Smith's drafting of the report for her subordinate enabled the patient to receive better treatment and maintain mental stability and avoid hospitalization. This is the polar opposite of "endangering the safety of others." (emphasis added)

To say Smith was upset is a great understatement . . . this was her integrity of 31 years assaulted and assaulted so unnecessarily. Her good-faith reputation and integrity were sullied; she experienced many sleepless nights.

In our defense preparation, badly needed humor was injected when

Smith brought to my office a Lynne Brown, the former Clinic Director of Cahaba Mental Health. For some reason we three found humor at frequent twists and turns, and the resulting laughter, sometimes deep in the belly, was needed to offset the tension.

Brown, like Smith an African American female in her mid-60s, had an expansive view of the Cahaba Mental Health employment arena. She helped us see the circumstantial nature, as well as the pattern and practice by Cahaba, of both our race and age discrimination claims in our federal court case.

Paragraph 13 of our federal discrimination lawsuit stated:

> This incident gave (the executive director) a surface excuse, though unjustified, to terminate Ms. Smith, and replace her with Ms. Hill, a much younger Caucasian, who is much less qualified for the position. Accordingly, CCMH's decision to terminate Ms. Smith further reflects a pattern and practice of race discrimination in employment decisions. CCMH's upper management is overwhelmingly Caucasian, and is in essence, a "sister-clique" of younger Caucasian females. CCMH's management's actions have overwhelmingly favored Caucasian employees, while subjecting African American employees to disparate treatment.

The "sister-clique" term extended back to a private high school in Selma, Morgan Academy, a then all-white privileged academy where three of the four Cahaba females whose depositions I took had all gone to school together. All three ladies came across professionally at their depositions, but all confirmed the elite whiteness of their socio-economic backgrounds.

Paragraphs 14–18 of Smith's federal discrimination lawsuit confirmed what was happening to older African Americans, mostly females, at Cahaba (CCMH) during the five-month period from October 2019 to February 2020:

> 14. Ms. Debra Evans, another older African American and former twenty-four (24) year employee of CCMH, was also terminated on or about October 7, 2019, for paperwork not being completed in a timely manner.

15. Mr. Tracy Vaughn, an African American male who had worked at CCMH for over ten (10) years, was terminated around February 2020. In addition, Ms. Lakeshia Harrison, an African American female, who had worked at CCMH for approximately sixteen (16) years, was terminated in February 2020.

16. In another incident, an African American employee was terminated as a result of a picture on her Facebook page. The employee did not post the picture herself, but it was posted by another individual.

17. Nonetheless, Ms. Tammy Till, a Caucasian female, was promoted to the Director of Developmental Disability Services position. This position was not posted, and Ms. Till did not have to interview for the job.

18. Further, Caucasian employees are allowed to regularly run personal errands while on the clock and/or travel to their homes. These employees include Billy Day and Lynne Sanders. Yet, African American employees are required to sign out when they leave the office, but Caucasian employees are not required to sign out.

In August 2021, I took depositions in Selma of four top Management officials at Cahaba Mental Health Center. I was pleased with the answers I obtained, as "hard to explain away" facts kept popping up. This was a case I was eager to try.

Discovery (the process of finding out additional information) can be hard work, and so it was here. We had not completed those August 2021 depositions when the defense counsel and I agreed to an informal resolution. Often, if a case is resolved, both sides agree to keep their terms confidential, and thus I will say no more.

However, a trial was avoided in both state and federal courts. My client Elizabeth Smith was happy to move on to the next phase of her life, wherever it might lead her. A happy client, to me, is the highest reward, and my client, in a spirit of forgiveness and reconciliation, today has goodwill again toward the Cahaba Mental Health Center, and the actual good work it often does. We wish it all the best in its professional future. We believe Cahaba learned something from Smith standing up to it and will deliver good services in the future to its clientele.

## 14

# Vanessa Dixon Defeats
# the Ku Klux Klan

This client ranks at the top of my list in the gratitude department. We have had many clients grateful for the good results obtained but Vanessa Dixon's heartfelt, genuine praise was music for my soul and deeply appreciated also by firm attorneys Chase Estes and David Sawyer.

Dixon was born on June 25, 1972, and adopted at age one by her grandmother's sister. She grew up in Montgomery while her adopted mom worked very hard to make ends meet.

Dixon is African American. She obtained a GED then started taking nursing classes and earned a Certified Nursing Assistant (CNA) status. Her duties were itinerant, traveling around helping the sick and elderly at their respective homes.

In June 1992, she married a fine young man, Tracey Lee Dixon, but he became super ill in 2017, requiring major surgery to remove tumors. Thank God, Dixon said, that her nursing education enabled her to save the medical expense by taking care of her husband herself. He recovered.

Eventually, to make ends meet, Dixon also started working for Don Terry Associates (DTA) at Baptist Hospital as a lower-level supervisor. She herself was injured falling down steps, which took her out of commission for a while. She applied for patrol work, picking up packages and delivering mail for DTA, which was less stressful than having to patrol all of Baptist Hospital.

In the midst of all this, Dixon was harassed by a white female supervisor at DTA. This upper-level supervisor even encouraged someone in Ku Klux Klan robes, with cone-head hood and eye openings to harass Dixon on the job. Dixon says she was "scared to death." This may have been a fun game for her supervisor and the Klan, but it was no fun for her. She had never been so scared. After Dixon complained, she was fired by DTA.

Lacking the resources and knowledge to seek an attorney, Dixon filed a *pro se* charge of race discrimination in June 2015. She finally obtained a right-to-sue letter in 2018 and then came to see our firm.

Knowing she had nothing to pay for our time, but having a heart for her ordeal, we took her case on a percentage. I assigned it to my associate Chase Estes, whom Dixon later described as "very caring" and "very nice." Estes prepared a decent lawsuit, but a summary judgment motion, filed by the defense, resulted in the court ruling in DTA's favor, and throwing the case out.

At that point, Estes was preparing to leave the McPhillips firm, so the persuasive Dixon convinced firm attorney David Sawyer, standing in our hallway, to represent her on appeal to the 11th Circuit U.S. Court of Appeals in Atlanta. That court is generally known for being quite conservative or pro-employer. But this time the higher court was more enlightened than the district court. And compassionate Sawyer, at little cost to the client, wrote one heck of a brief.

"Thanks be to God" was Dixon's reaction when she won at the 11th Circuit. That victory was a result of Sawyer's excellent work product, and she and I congratulated him for his stellar work.

But this only sent us back to the U.S. District Court for a trial in front of Judge Austin Huffaker, a judge whom I greatly respect.

So, Sawyer and I together started preparing for a spring 2022 trial.

Meanwhile, attorney Welsey Pitters, an African American, originally from Jamaica, started defending DTA. I respect Pitters, but we had very different views about the merits of the case, and Dixon and we weren't going to settle for something minimal. So, back and forth we went, and throughout the process, my appreciation grew for Dixon, and her courage and perseverance.

When cases of this sort are resolved, it is almost always on a confidential basis, and this was no exception. Thus, this case was amicably and satisfactorily resolved in April 2022, weeks before the trial.

We had a happy client who felt justice was achieved, especially against the Klan, something you do not expect to see or hear about in a majority Black city like Montgomery, at least as recently as 2015, and in a city now with a Black mayor.

What truly warmed my heart in the end was that this client, Vanessa Dixon, was deeply grateful for all we did to help her, from Chase Estes, to David Sawyer, to me, and to Amy Strickland and Cesaire McPherson. Dixon also reminded me that I had prayed with her and her husband several times, for illnesses, and the results had always been good. In the end, she said that our kindness sent chills up and down her arms. Such an expression meant more to me than any amount of money.

It was also good to send another bully, especially the Klan, into retreat.

## 15

# Insurance Companies Can Also Bully

Our law firm interacts with insurance companies every day. Usually, it is because the company is insuring some person or business against liability caused by an accident, negligence, or breach of contract. A good insurance policy comes with a healthy premium but pays for legal representation and any damages arising from a settlement or court judgment.

Sometimes the contact is more adversarial, as when insurance fails to pay a claim, or the company terminates its own employee, and/or wrongfully discriminates against him or her based on race, sex, age, national origin, religion, or disability, in violation of federal law.

That happened with Jennifer Akridge when ALFA Mutual Insurance Company wrongfully terminated her in December 2016. Her terrible sin? That she dared develop multiple sclerosis, which allowed her health insurance costs to higher than the self-insured ALFA wanted to pay. Of course, ALFA disagreed, but our successful appeal to the 11th Circuit U.S. Court of Appeals, rendered in June 2021, strengthened our hand. See *Akridge vs. Alfa*, 1 F.4 1271 (11th C. 2021) (see also Chapter 19 of *Only in Alabama*, discussing the grave injustice rendered by young U.S. Magistrate Judge Gray Borden granting summary, before the 11th Circuit reversed).

This tells the story about another Alabama insurance company wrongfully terminating its own employee, in an extremely unfair way. However, due to the company's insistence at settlement of certain non-disparagement language by my client in the agreement, I have given fictitious names to the insurance company and my client, the aggrieved employee. We have also shifted the location of the business, to disguise the guilty and protect the innocent.

Therefore, we rename the employee "Constance Reynolds" and call the insurance company, "Appalachian Insurance Mutual (AIM)."

Otherwise, the circumstances closely resemble the true-life story. The real culprit can remain in hiding, thanks to a substantial settlement otherwise unrevealed.

For me, the story began when Reynolds came to see me in July 2018. Still in her middle years, she had developed a good career as a salesperson for the insurance company, signing up many new clients. She had received promotions, raises, and bonuses, all well-deserved. She had a good reputation.

Reynolds was attractive with a sparkling personality. She had chosen to remain single, but that didn't stop her from adopting a young mixed-race son, with mild autistic tendencies.

Reynolds shared with me how the company's Birmingham location had grown into a highly male-dominated "macho type" of office. The president of AIM we'll call Michael Brooks. He was often overly flirtatious. He frequently bragged about his hunting accomplishments and successes in other male-dominated activities. But Reynolds was never invited to participate in any of these so-called business trips. Only male employees were invited to deep-sea fishing trips and out-of-state entertainment centers.

My client innocently asked why she was never included in these trips. Her boss's standard response was "Oh, you would not want to go on this trip," as though it was funny that she, a single female, would even think about such a trip.

That wasn't all. President Brooks continually questioned Reynolds about her love life, wanting to know more details about who she was dating. Reynolds would diplomatically fend off such questions from her boss. A married man, Brooks constantly complimented Reynolds about her appearance, but never made similar comments to male employees.

Although the comments made Reynolds uncomfortable, she tried to stay "under the radar." Her job as a salesperson allowed her to travel around the state. When she was gone, CEO Brooks directed his attention toward other younger single females in the office.

Occasionally, unable to resist the pressure, Reynolds would cave in and give the name of someone she was dating. Unfortunately, that only made matters worse, with her boss pressing to know more. Was it curiosity, jealousy, or something else?

I initially assisted Reynolds in filing an EEOC charge on sex discrimination only. However, we deliberately let her right-to-sue time run out, because AIM, trying to fend off a suit, was suddenly treating her much better. They also knew I was her attorney.

Then, without warning, only a few days after she let her first EEOC right-to-sue time expire, Reynolds was notified she was being terminated. She was given no reason for her termination. Accordingly, she wasted no time in letting her bosses know that "Julian McPhillips was still her attorney." Her words, not mine.

Shortly thereafter, the insurance company's counsel sent me a "separation agreement and general release" for my client to sign. Then I received an email from AIM's attorneys, stating that Reynolds's termination was "due to her spending unauthorized company money on meals," while on the road, soliciting business for AIM.

This seemed like a very weak excuse to me and a nonexistent reason to my client. In the legal business we call this "pretextual," meaning "not the real reason." Reynolds's reply to me, and my reply to AIM, was that my client was actually entitled to be reimbursed by AIM, since she was out on the road working for AIM, visiting existing customers, to firm them up, or seeking new business for AIM.

Not surprisingly, Reynolds's former job was soon handed to a young white male with no previous sales or insurance experience. He didn't even have an insurance license when hired.

Accordingly, Reynolds, with my assistance, wasted no time in filing a second sex discrimination charge with the Equal Employment Opportunity Commission in Birmingham (EEOC). This time, however, we also filed a wrongful retaliation charge.

As is usually the mode in EEOC investigations, the case "rocked on" for the next eight months, meaning that nothing happened. The EEOC investigators are typically overwhelmed with hundreds of cases to research, and woefully inadequate time to do so.

The EEOC, however, after 180 days of investigation, routinely gives a complaining party a "right-to-sue" good for 90 days, once awarded. Thus Reynolds eventually received a second right-to-sue, and this time we prepared a well-drafted lawsuit.

I took some aggressive depositions of Brooks and several other employees, and associate attorney Chase Estes provided excellent leadership in drafting our brief to help defend against an adverse ruling by a federal judge on the insurance company's summary judgment motion. Had we lost that ruling, we'd have been thrown out of court. We had two very talented law firms working against us, one from Birmingham, the other from Montgomery. Fortunately, the federal judge ruled in our favor on the wrongful retaliation claim. The trial was drawing near.

Long story short, while still in the pandemic, our case was set for trial in December 2021. Having already tried three jury trials in 2021 (two criminal, one civil, with good results in two), I was super psyched up about trying my fourth jury trial in one year, notwithstanding undesirable mask requirements.

At the last moment, however, the attorneys on both sides agreed with our clients that mediation was worth trying, and so we did. Although the agreement was subject to confidentiality, it is fair to say, since the parties' names and location have been changed, that a substantial result for my clients was achieved. I wish I could share more about the number.

In the process not only was a victory for Reynolds achieved, but it was also a major victory for civil justice. In the insurance company's world, this outcome rang loudly like a bell, warning bosses not to sexually harass and not to retaliate against an employee filing an EEOC charge.

## 16

# Grove Park Jungle Restored

This story belongs in a book about bullies. Who was the bully, and who were the victims? You, the readers, must answer those questions. This is about a piece of Montgomery's history worth preserving. My close proximity across 44 years (1978 to 2022) gave me a bird's eye view to the location in despair. I participated in the continuing saga, both as attorney and property owner.

I first noticed this controversial complex known as "The Grove Court Apartments" in 1978. That was after I accepted attorney Tommy Gallion's invitation to move into his building at 516 S. Perry Street in Montgomery. The alleyway behind Tommy's building turned off Grove Street, adjacent to the apartments. In my early days, a few tenants hung out on the balconies, with music blaring.

I noticed nothing historical about these apartments. They were built as early as one year after my birth. That didn't seem enough to be historical in age standards. In 2020, my friend, attorney Billy Hill, eight years older, told me he played as a kid in a sand pile outside the apartments' 1947 construction.

By the mid-1980s, the apartments were abandoned and overgrown. Birds and other critters made the site seem ghostly and dangerous. In 1982, upon purchasing my office building from Gallion's in-laws, I started parking in front of the office, on Perry Street, away from the apartments' eyesore.

As the 1980s moved into the 1990s and bounced into the 2000s, other Perry Street denizens complained to me about the dilapidated monstrosity behind my offices. The Grove Court complex disintegrated into an ugly mess. It looked like bombed-out Germany after World War II. Tenants had been robbed in the area. At night, especially on dark cold winter days, the location scared off our female office workers, requiring us to add outside lights.

Complaining owner-neighbors included prominent realtors Jim Inscoe and Carlyle Chandler; businessman Al Wade; attorneys Richard Moxley and Richard Shinbaum; and Ginger Avery, executive director of the Alabama Association of Justice, and her largely female staff.

City Councilman Tracy Larkin and Montgomery County Commissioner Isaiah Sankey were also upset and became my strong allies. The apartments were a tremendous eyesore, and a hangout for criminals and vagrants, with offensive graffiti. Had a fire broken out, the asbestos in the smoke and fumes would have unleashed dangerous air for people, including my own office personnel, to breathe.

By the late 1990s and 2000s I had a thick file. I found a December 20, 2007, letter sent to then-Mayor Bobby Bright, requesting "assistance to remove this horrible blight from our neighborhood. It dragged down neighborhood property values and threatened the safety of Montgomery citizens." The absentee owners of the apartments were two Abraham brothers, but their home addresses could never be found. Reportedly they were in South Florida at an undeliverable address.

Nothing happened for decades, Todd Strange succeeded Bobby Bright as mayor in 2004. Letters sent in 2013 to Mayor Strange generated only expressions of sympathy, as with Bobby Bright. The City of Montgomery, which often threatened landowners of abandoned properties with demolition, apparently concluded that the cost of removal of the Grove Court complex was too expensive given its mass of concrete and metal.

As we moved into 2018–2019, I was contacted by neighbors, especially business owners down the street, unhappy with the city's "do nothing" attitude. Neighbor Richard Shinbaum was the most helpful. We decided it was time to do something substantial. So we co-drafted a lawsuit. Overwhelmed at times by his bankruptcy law practice, Shinbaum was content to let me take the lead. I did so with help from office manager Amy Strickland.

I sent three letters to newly elected Mayor Steve Reed in 2018–2019, seeking assistance before filing suit. Steve's father, the powerful

Democratic political boss Joe Reed, gave me much credit for helping his son get elected probate judge in 2012. That became a springboard for Steven Reed's election to mayor in 2018. Much to my dismay, there was no reply from Reed to my three letters. In hindsight, I realize Reed had other friends, "historic preservationists." Yet I consider myself a preservationist, having saved three houses in Old Cloverdale, especially the renowned Fitzgerald Museum house. Nonetheless, I felt Reed owed me the simple courtesy of a reply, even if he disagreed with me. The young mayor never replied.

I went to the Montgomery City Council meeting to speak to its members on its November 2019 agenda. Present were City Council President Charles Jinright and council members Tracy Larkin, Arch Lee, Richard Bollinger, Brantly Lyons, Audrey Graham, William Green, Fred Bell, and Glenn Pruitt. No one expressed any words of opposition. Jinright piped up in a whisperingly low tone and said, "We all agree with you."

Thanks. Agreement is one thing. Action is another. I have learned this the hard way over the years, especially in cases with the City of Montgomery. Montgomery is one of the few totally self-insured municipalities in Alabama, believing it can save more money that way.

I kept the neighborhood owners on South Perry Street aware of our lack of progress from the city mayor's office. We all bent over backwards to motivate the city to do something meaningful, either tear down and remove this ugly monstrosity, or somehow find a buyer to restore it. Upon no reply from Mayor Reed, after repeated attempts, we were tired of the "big run-around."

Reflecting the gross hypocrisy of the City of Montgomery was a newspaper article with a picture in the Sunday, December 15, 2019, edition of *Montgomery Advertiser*. The headline read: "Montgomery Woman Claims City Unfairly Demolished Her Family's 100-year-old Home."

No cooperation or even communication came from the city. Neighborhood business owners and I concluded we had gone the extra mile, and that we had no alternative but to file suit. A well-researched, well-pled complaint for injunction was prepared, seeking equitable relief against both the City of Montgomery and the Grove Court Apartments, Inc. The

$756 filing fee was shared equally by the various neighborhood plaintiffs, including me.

A lawsuit was filed on February 14, 2020, and served on the City of Montgomery. We attached the January 7, 2020, front page story from the *Montgomery Advertiser* with a picture of Mayor Reed and the title of the column: "Reed's transition teams want to hear from you." Written on the photocopy in handwriting by me were words encouraging Mayor Reed to reply so a suit would be unnecessary. I also attached the article about the lady's 100-year-old home being demolished by the city, despite her objections.

Did we get any further response from Mayor Reed or any one of his assistants? Absolutely not!

For all five co-plaintiffs, our consciences were clear. Reed left us no choice. We set forth the history of the apartment's abandonment for 35 years and stated that it was an eyesore and public nuisance, with people mugged, and a threat to the health and safety of citizens of Montgomery. We also cited several city ordinances giving the City of Montgomery the power to punish ineffective landlords. We cited other ordinances requiring the city to remove overgrown weeds and all the litter, trash, stagnant water, abandoned vehicles, etc.

We also cited a city ordinance allowing the city to close condemned vacant structures unfit for human habitation and occupancy. We cited the Code of Alabama section authorizing immediate demolition of unsafe structures. We said the City of Montgomery's lack of action was negligent, reckless, and wanton. We set forth how the Montgomery City Council members, especially Tracy Larkin and Steve Bollinger, had pushed the city to do what we were requesting, and how the city failed to honor their requests. Unfortunately, Larkin and Bollinger both died in 2019–2020. We missed their friendship, help, and leadership.

Shortly thereafter, County Commissioner Isaiah Sankey, in whose district the apartments are located, filed a motion to intervene on our side, and we resumed our old friendship with him.

Our lawsuit stated the Grove Court Apartments were not listed on the National Register of Historic places until December 2013, long after their abandonment. This was after they had become a nuisance. We stated this listing was a last-ditch effort in 2013. It prevented demolition—not allowing us to obtain federal funds—to gain advantage for a potential purchaser.

We also expressed to the Court that the prior owners in the Abraham Estate were called upon by the City of Montgomery to repair or remove the property. Unfortunately, they never did so. The Abraham brothers, before or after their deaths, allowed the deteriorated property to be owned by Grove Court Apartments, Inc. Its stock ownership was unknown.

Co-Counsel Richard Shinbaum knew the Abraham family personally through local synagogue contacts. He was on the trail of helping us locate and serve the owners of the corporation. Well into the pandemic era, we participated in several Zoom motion hearings with city defense attorney Chris East. He was ably defending the case before Montgomery Circuit Judge Brooke Reid. She was helpful, but also frustrated, as were we, in getting the owners to respond.

The City of Montgomery was understandably reluctant to pay $2 million in estimated costs to remove all the concrete, metal, asbestos, and debris. The city stood to benefit, however.

As litigation continued through the pandemic years of 2020–2021, I conferred with my good friend Randall Williams, owner of NewSouth Books and publisher of this book. Randall respectfully explained his different view. He said the architecture, combined with concrete and metal, had a unique historical design that was not existent elsewhere in Alabama.

Long story short, Williams called me a few months later, in the spring of 2021. He informed me his good friend Tom Blount, the second-oldest son of the late famous entrepreneur-philanthropist Winton M. "Red" Blount, had purchased the Grove Court Apartments. The younger Blount, a year older than me at 76, would be spending millions to renovate the apartments and transform them into new usefulness. I talked personally with Blount and confirm the sincerity and depth of his commitment. He already had homes in Los Angeles and Italy and was finishing a major renovation of long-vacant buildings on Commerce Street downtown (those are now the beautiful and successful Ravello restaurant complex).

Blount was fully committed to this expansive new project of Grove

Court Apartments in his childhood hometown. Blount's legacy gift to Montgomery would be similar in spirit to his father's enormous legacy gift of the Alabama Shakespeare Theater and Blount Cultural Park.

With this solid assurance and cooperation, Tom Blount intervened in the lawsuit. We voluntarily agreed to discontinue the litigation, while maintaining the right to resurrect it if Blount's commitment later faltered.

I later told Randall Williams, the real "unsung hero" of this saga, that he had helped save this property. I thanked my longtime friend. He deserves great recognition, and I thank my friend Tom Blount for stepping up when no one else had done so.

In the late spring and summer of 2021, the Grove Court Apartments received an initial facelift to remove overgrown vegetation, debris, and other evidence of dereliction, including some squatters. In mid-September 2021, Montgomery's Landmarks Foundation held one of its "Renovator's Open House" receptions to let interested persons see the work that was planned and being done. Blount's nephew, Jud Blount, explained his uncle's plans. Jud is involved with the repair, reconstruction, and development of the long-abandoned monstrosity.

Richard Shinbaum and I were also left smiling. We believed our litigation helped the ultimate outcome. We await the finished product. Hopefully, this bully is tamed.

Meanwhile, Blount has had teams of architects and workers drawing new interior and landscaping plans, putting on new roofs, readying the openings for new windows, doors, and mechanical systems, sandblasting the exterior so it can be painted, and all the other countless details of such a massive rehabilitation project. Much more work remains to be done and it may be a couple of years before the units are ready for occupancy.

# Roy Moore Vindicated

A twist of the famous Shakespearean title—"Too much ado about everything"—is an appropriate way to start this chapter. This case was one for the history books, legal journals, psychology books, theology magazines, and political commentaries. Throw in pride and prejudice, unforgiveness, and illicit opportunity. You will have a barnburner of a story.

This is such a story. It involves the how, the why, the wherefores, and the scruples, or lack thereof, of a supposed victim of sexual harassment, who was just waiting 40 years later to reveal her story. This was just 32 days before a December 2017 U.S. Senate special election date. Yet, when Roy Moore, the alleged culprit, denied her false allegations, the alleged victim sued him for defamation for his mere denial.

Does that sound fair?

Who is really the bully? This is especially true when the famous accuser is backed by multi-million-dollar resources from an unnamed secret source, with lawyers flying in from San Francisco, New York, and Washington. Who? Not Roy Moore. But who?

In my own five-plus decades of lawyering in New York and Alabama, I'd never seen anything like it. I hope never to again. Also, I must be careful in how I write this; I don't want to get sued myself for defamation.

So, who are we talking about? Her name was Leigh Corfman. She says that at age fourteen and a half in 1978 she was sexually abused by Roy Moore, then a 32-year-old deputy district attorney in Etowah County (Gadsden). Moore adamantly and vehemently denied it, emphasizing that in his seven subsequent Alabama election races, five for state office, and two for the county, there never had been a hint, rumor, or suggestion of any sexual impropriety by himself. That was during the period 1982 to 2012.

In 2017, this 40-year-old sexual molestation charge jumped out on candidate Moore. It was like an octopus sucking blood. It couldn't have been more strategically and devastatingly harmful, wounding Moore irreparably in the election. This surprised candidate went from 11 points ahead in statewide polls to losing by one point to Democrat Doug Jones in an intensely red state.

The "sexual harassment" charge had morphed into "sexual molestation." That certainly sounds much worse. The charge clearly cost Moore the election. It also deeply hurt him, his wife Kayla, and his family personally.

In Chapter 14 of *Only in Alabama*, I described how I first came to know Roy Moore. It was against my Democratic grain to say so. However, despite disagreement on key issues such as gun control laws, I stated that Moore had been dealt an enormous wrong by the media. Rather than rehash how that affected the election of 2017, this chapter instead addresses the intrigue of the lawsuit itself.

When the election was over in December 2017, both Moore and Corfman were feeling bruised and bloodied. She and her supporting cast, including the *Washington Post*, had succeeded in making Roy Moore look like a pedophile. It also painted Moore as a tremendous hypocrite, especially in light of his strong moral stand for the Ten Commandments and against abortion and same-sex marriage. "Judge," as Moore was called during the campaign, was ridiculed unmercifully by certain interests, especially the political left. Moore and his wife Kayla were subjected to vicious, unrelenting attacks, via social media, emails, and public newscast attacks. Moore was "tarred and feathered" by columnists including John Archibald of AL.com, who won a Pulitzer Prize. The *Birmingham News* had a field day, as did all the state's newspapers.

Meanwhile, Corfman was lionized by *Time* magazine as "Person of the Year." She was invited by NBC's Today Show to fly to New York at its expense. She was interviewed by the famous Savannah Guthrie. Corfman's name was portrayed heroically from coast to coast. She was ballyhooed by both the national and international press.

Corfman obviously enjoyed all the attention. She wasted no time keeping her name in the limelight by filing a lawsuit against Roy Moore for defamation only weeks after the election was over, in early January 2018.

Back in the Etowah County home base for both Corfman and Moore. Corfman deservedly received ample negative feedback. That was her stated rationale for suing Moore. She said it was her reputation, now "tarnished" by Moore's denials of her sexual molestation charge against him. That primarily consisted of his touching her on the outside of her bra. Corfman listed numerous campaign speeches where Moore described 40-year-old charges as "false and malicious." This adamant denial became the basis for her defamation lawsuit. Moore had carefully avoided mentioning Corfman's name. Moore also refrained from calling Corfman "a liar," a fact conceded by her litigation team.

During 2018–2019, before the pandemic began, Moore called me to help him on the venue issue—what county the lawsuit should be filed in. He wanted the case moved to Etowah County, northeast of Birmingham. This was the home of both Moore and Corfman. It was also where the alleged incidents took place. My law partner Kenneth Shinbaum and I worked together on that goal. Unfortunately, the Alabama Supreme Court kept the case in Montgomery County, not Etowah?

With much more limited resources than the Corfman team suing him, Moore wisely decided to let Melissa Isaak, 42, a very competent female attorney, develop the rest of his defense. It flowed through the courts over the next four years, 2018–2022. Depositions were taken in California, Ohio, Florida, North Carolina, and Montgomery and Gadsden. At Moore's request, due to his modest financial situation, I stayed on the sidelines, but refrained from withdrawing as his attorney of record.

Then, in mid-November 2021, Moore called and asked me to return. He said the size of the case was overwhelming Isaak. She also called and requested that I come back in, humbly admitting she had never been in a jury trial before and, given the size and depth of the resources on Corfman's legal team, the case would be best suited with two counsel. Isaak's primary field was divorce law. Her specialty was representing only men. Originally from North Dakota, she was now married to an Alabama man she had met at Fort Rucker. Issak had done a good but exhausting job on the pre-trial discovery. She had single-handedly responded to Corfman's large team of competent attorneys. They were funded by who knows whom.

Jumping back in, I scrambled through a pile of depositions. I visited Moore several times at his Dexter Avenue office—the "Foundation for Moral Law"—in downtown Montgomery. I even saw the famous Ten Commandments Monument for the first time.

A serious question was raised in my book, *Only in Alabama*: "*How could a woman of such modest means afford to pay for two attorneys flying in from San Francisco and another attorney coming down from New York.* Was this for a simple venue hearing in April 2018?" From there Corfman's support team grew to include three sharp, veteran attorneys, including the famous Lightfoot Franklin firm in Birmingham, namely Harlan Prater, Melody Eagan, and Jeff Doss. The kingpin attorney orchestrating both the legal and public relations aspects was none other than renowned attorney Neil Roman of the nationally powerful Washington, D.C., law firm of Covington and Burling. Roman had reportedly associated with Karl Rove, the alleged behind-the-scenes manipulator in the Don Siegelman prosecution.

Roman's name was blurted out by Corfman in her testimony about how the sexual harassment story began in 2017. That meant that Roman actually should have been listed as a witness by both Corfman and Moore. He seemed much involved in the *Washington Post* story, which only partially explains his leadership in the end.

The jury returned a favorable verdict for Roy Moore on February 2, 2022. They concluded he had not defamed Corfman. That seemed to shock Corfman and her high-powered team. Roman spoke to the press at the courthouse after the verdict. He tried to spin the jury's denial of Corfman's claims against Moore. While speaking, Roman was surrounded by a team of eight to ten staffers. That included three more attorneys, for a total of six, most with disappointed expressions on their faces. They had expected a victory; unfortunately for them, their monumental effort over four years didn't produce one.

The big question again was where did all this money come from? This big fat question still evades answer. The Corfman legal team filed a motion in limine to prevent this issue from even being raised at trial, and Judge

John Rochester granted it. The enormous disparity of resources in favor of Corfman strangely made Moore look like "David" and Corfman like "Goliath" in the January–February 2022 trial. This was despite a public image to the contrary.

Who was Judge Rochester? He was not a Montgomery County Circuit Judge. He was instead appointed by Acting Chief Justice Lynn Stuart after the original judge, Roman Shaul, resigned his position as circuit judge. Montgomery's next judge, Jimmy Pool, recused himself, followed by all other Montgomery Circuit Court Judges. Judge Rochester is from Clay County, two counties northeast of Montgomery. I met him in 1977, while I was beginning my own campaign for Alabama attorney general, following two years as assistant attorney general. I have always enjoyed a good rapport with Judge Rochester but had had less contact in recent years.

Moore and Isaak had earlier unsuccessfully tried to get Rochester to recuse himself due to his monetary support of Doug Jones in the 2017 U.S. Senate race, but Rochester had refused. My reentering the case, with a preexisting friendship with Judge Rochester, definitely helped Moore.

Two weeks before the January 24, 2022, trial date, Moore discovered a 1979–1980 Polaroid picture of his backwoods home in Gallant in Etowah County. We passed it on to Corfman's lawyer, Melody Eagan, who pitched a fit. She claimed it was deliberately hidden. Melody also insisted on taking Moore's deposition a third time, and we acquiesced. It gave me a chance to see Eagan's steel-trap mind at work. She was tough.

## THE TRIAL

Let's talk about what happened at the 2022 trial, which began on January 24 and ended nine days later, on February 2. I was not surprised that the attorneys were given a jury panel to choose from that was 72.3 percent African American, with the rest Caucasian, and a few Asian. The demographics of Montgomery had been changing for years. Given the overwhelming high Black vote for Doug Jones in the 2017 election, this looked ominous for Roy Moore. Frankly, I was comfortable with those percentages, as both my law practice and Democratic political life in several state-wide and county delegate elections over 47 years had enhanced my own reputation in the Black community of Montgomery County.

In voir dire, the process of choosing a jury, I shared my own Democratic credentials and civil rights orientation. Several jurors, black and white, said they knew about me. They were quickly struck by Corfman's team, which included the brilliant Jeff Doss, a middle-aged attorney who knew my daughter Grace in the 1990s at St. James School in Montgomery. Jeff did a voir dire presentation for Corfman, mocking Roy Moore's twice removal from the Alabama Supreme Court in the preamble of his questions. Doss further primed the jurors with questions as to their memories about accusations against Moore from Corfman and other women during the 2017 campaign. Approximately 20 of the 50 jurors on our panel said they remembered. Doss did all he could to impugn Moore's character before the entire panel.

The lawyers and judge agreed that four alternate jurors would be picked in addition to 12 regular jurors, due to the still-threatening Covid. Indeed, we were the first and only jury trial happening in the Montgomery County Courthouse for January 2022. The powers that be at said courthouse must have figured that the four years and one month since the suit was filed, plus the newsworthy nature of it, bumped our case to the front of the line, ahead of the many other still-pending jury trials, including criminal.

We ended up with 16 jurors—15 African Americans and one Caucasian, an 89-year-old man. I was accurately quoted the next day that I was pleased with the majority Black jury: "We think the African Americans here are sick and tired of this kind of injustice [Moore's] been subjected to."

Roy Moore added that his goal was simply to have the truth come out.

The 89-year-old juror, about whom I was earlier leery due to his membership in the ultra-liberal Immanuel Presbyterian Church in east Montgomery, was removed as a juror due to improper contact with a Corfman expert witness at the elevator. A Black female juror was also removed due to medical issues. That left us with 14 African American jurors, including two alternates.

Due to their burden of proof, Corfman's lawyers were allowed to go first. In opening statements, they showed Moore addressing a question about Barack Obama's citizenship. It had nothing to do with the case except as an attempt to prejudice the jury. The plaintiff's team then laid it on us thick by calling many now older female witnesses. Most testified by deposition against Roy Moore. They didn't hurt Moore that much, as no one but Corfman would confirm any sexual harassment by Roy Moore. No one saw Moore do anything to Corfman. Her case was largely one of conjecture, inference, exaggeration, and hyperbole. Not surprising!

Our tactic was to portray Corfman as motivated by her desire to remain in "the limelight," with interviews and TV appearances on NBC's Today Show with the famous Savannah Guthrie. Corfman had received unending, ego-feeding praise from the many Democrats and anti-Moore Republicans pleased by Moore's defeat. Corfman hungrily desired more of this, explaining her firing the first shot with the defamation lawsuit against Moore.

We knew Corfman had ample encouragement and support from those opposing Moore's views on moral issues—the Ten Commandments; abortion; and same-sex marriage. However, she was also backed by Big Business and Big Insurance interests unhappy with Moore's pro-consumer, pro-little man, civil justice views. After all, I knew that Judge Bob Vance Jr., a former political opponent of Moore, had described Moore as having the "biggest heart for the little guy by far" of the nine Republican justices, on both civil and criminal issues. We regretted not calling Judge Vance as a witness at trial, and I never quoted him at trial.

Corfman and her legal team hoped to gain tactical advantage with the jury by announcing they were not seeking financial damages but only a declaratory judgment. She said "that Moore's denials had "defamed" her." Corfman had earlier withdrawn her initial request for a public apology, something the law could not enforce.

We argued in return that if Corfman were not damaged, she would therefore not be defamed, because to be defamed, one has to be damaged.

At the trial's beginning, Judge Rochester again denied our motion for a directed verdict on the grounds of Moore's qualified privilege to deny a false charge without defamation exposure. We also argued that truth and opinion were absolute defenses, and that is what Moore spoke about Corfman was not only true but was Moore's opinion.

Day two of the trial was January 25, 2022, which began with Corfman's team, consisting of at least five lawyers and four technical assistants, presenting their case.

The plaintiff's first witness was her own mother, Nancy Wells, to help bolster Corfman's story about meeting Roy Moore at the Etowah County Courthouse in Gadsden in February 1979. Wells first admitted, however, that she gave up custody of her daughter at 14 years of age that year because of too many problems, including the daughter falsely changing a grade on her report card and staying out too late at night with friends. The mother also acknowledged that Corfman never told her about any sexual contact with Roy Moore until many years later.

The next witness was Leigh Corfman herself. She claimed Moore took her to his home twice, and that the second time Moore touched her on the outside of her bra. As to this terrible "child molestation" charge, Corfman admitted she waited until 40 years later to reveal it. Corfman, to her credit, admitted the multiple failed marriages and bankruptcies she had experienced, and that she wasn't proud of much of her past. It was as if Roy Moore had somehow caused this, too.

Isaak's cross-examination of Corfman was a work of art! Isaak showed how Corfman wasn't just the innocent little victim who, against her wishes, got pulled into the controversy. Instead, questioning Corfman from text messages with a *Washington Post* reporter, Melissa brought out that Corfman had long been planning this attack, working with others on strategic timing. Corfman admitted to Melissa she texted a friend before the *Washington Post* story broke, "Let the games begin . . . " Corfman also confirmed that she gave the *Post* reporter a list of other names for the reporter to contact. All this made Corfman look manipulative and aggressive, which she was, and that didn't sit well with the jury, in my opinion. Isaak also brought out the name of Richard Hagedorn, painting him as a co-conspirator working with Corfman. Hagedorn wasn't happy that Roy Moore, as a circuit judge, had held [Hagedorn] in contempt of court for nonpayment of child support in 1990.

Isaak also got Corfman to admit that she publicly, in front of many people, at an accident location in May 2021, blurted out her name, excitedly and repeatedly saying that: "I am the Roy Moore accuser." This reinforced our "limelight" motivation defense to Corfman's false accusations.

The so-called list of other women, put on mostly by video, was largely weak and ineffective. None had ever seen Moore do anything themselves, or they only heard about Corfman's experience years later, or had a very limited relationship with Roy Moore themselves, at the age of 18–19.

Corfman's lawyers rested on the fourth day of trial, January 27, 2022, I immediately moved for a directed verdict for Moore on multiple defamation law grounds, but Judge Rochester again denied the same.

Kayla Moore, Roy's loyal wife, was our defense witness number one, and she was a star. She was humbly effective. In tears she described what a perfect gentleman Moore had been with her ever since their marriage in 1985. Kayla added that Roy had been a model husband and model father. She shared her husband's belief that the allegations were "politically motivated," stating that one of the female witnesses for Corfman had a sister "who is a lesbian and against my husband."

Kayla also testified how she and her husband had received death threats and many threatening or highly insulting text messages. Also, someone had spray-painted in large orange letters the words "pedophile" on the road leading to the Moores' home in Etowah County.

Our next witness was Moore's daughter, Heather Mayo. She emotionally echoed what her mother said. The next day, at least seven more female witnesses from Moore's hometown of Gallant or nearby Gadsden testified about Moore's good character. None of these witnesses had ever heard of any improper sexual allegations by anyone against Moore, except for Corfman.

Moore also had four male character witnesses, including Willie James and Leonard Holyfield, two African American men he had appointed or hired. The latter, from Atlanta, was a distant cousin of boxing champion Evander Holyfield. Both spoke boldly about Moore's civil rights sensitivity, his deep spirituality, and his leadership. Another witness from Mobile, Jimmy Flanagan, chief of police of the Alabama Port Authority, spoke glowingly of Moore's good character.

Our last witness was Roy Moore himself. I led him carefully with prompting questions. He testified how he carefully did not call Corfman "a liar" but acknowledged that he used strong language in describing Corfman's allegations, as "false and malicious." Moore held his ground, saying he had a right to deny someone else's false allegations.

The most poignant part of the trial may have been my walking Moore through about 50 social media messages and emails accusing him of having sex with his own son or daughter or doing other similar dangerous things as a pedophile. Moore humbly restrained himself and painfully acknowledged having received such texts from various anonymous sources. The courtroom was so silent because everyone was listening carefully, and you could have heard a pin drop. This was helpful to Moore because it seemed the jury gained sympathy for him for the pain and suffering endured by him and his wife caused by Corfman's allegations.

Moore also described his time on the Alabama Supreme Court, his reverence for the Ten Commandments, and, quite glaringly, insisted that "I never met that woman [referring to Corfman] until the first day of trial."

Moore also spoke glowingly about how, at the University of Alabama Law School, he was instrumental in drawing up Alabama's first Child Abuse law in 1977. He added that, in the early 1980s, in Gadsden, he prosecuted a prominent child abuse case, the first in Alabama under the new law he helped draft.

During closing arguments, I was attacked by Melody Eagan for downplaying what, if anything, Moore had done to Corfman. In closing I said that Judge Moore vehemently denied that anything happened sexually between him and Corfman. Nonetheless, if someone believed her, it was comparatively "child's play" (touching the outside of her bra) compared to what Presidents Clinton and Trump were each accused of doing to multiple women. Sharing the closing as well as the opening, Isaak and I knocked home many other favorable points for Moore.

The jury retired for one hour late Tuesday afternoon, February 1, 2022. They returned the next morning and two hours later announced they had reached a verdict.

Judge Rochester read: "On the plaintiff (Corfman's) claim that Roy

Moore defamed her, the jury found against Corfman and for Moore." My nervous heart breathed a huge sigh of relief. Then Rochester further read that as to Moore's counterclaim that Corfman had defamed him, the jury denied that. This was a verdict we had long anticipated, and we believed such a verdict would be a big victory for Roy Moore, as indeed it was.

Outside the courtroom, the press asked me for comment, and I replied, "I can't tell you, Mr. Moore, how proud I am of you and proud I am of Kayla to stand up to this junk, the bad things they've said about you all these past four years; you are completely vindicated."

After first giving God honor and thankfulness for His help, Moore also claimed it as a "huge victory" and "complete vindication." He added, "after all, [Corfman] started all this by suing me, not vice-versa."

Neil Roman, Corfman's attorney and P.R. Specialist, started scrambling and attempted to put a different spin on the outcome. He admitted they were all disappointed by the jury's verdict.

This was a verdict for justice. With this heavy hammer no longer hanging over their heads, Roy and Kayla left the courthouse with heads high, burdens lifted, and spirits rejuvenated.

For me and co-counsel Melissa Isaak, this representation was a highlight of our careers. It was honorable legal service for which we all express to God our gratitude.

*18*

# Travis Thomas Takes on Auburn

No more decent client of mine ever emerged from more humble circumstances than did Travis S. Thomas Sr.

## BACKGROUND

Born on October 9, 1984, Thomas was orphaned at age five after his
biological father intentionally ran over his mother in an automobile and
then shot her (she died a year later). The father later took his own life by
hanging himself in prison.

Young Travis was only four when his grandmother took over guard-
ianship of Travis, his two-year-old sister, and his wounded mother. Travis
was raised in Tuskegee and graduated from Booker T. Washington High
School.

Despite all this, Thomas was a good athlete, played football and also
had a keen intellect, and good character. He was soon attracted to the
field of athletic administration. By 2011 he had earned a bachelor's degree
in Sports Leadership from Auburn University Montgomery (AUM), and
by 2013, a master's degree in Exercise Physiology from the same school.
Thomas topped it off in 2019 with a second master's degree in Sports
Management, also from AUM.

Along the way he enjoyed a great professional experience at the University of Alabama (2012–2013, 2015–2016) and at Old Dominion University (2016–2017). Thomas was hired by Auburn University in May 2017,
initially as an academic counselor for swimming, diving, and volleyball.

## RELATIONSHIP AND SKILLS

Thomas's relationship skills with students were noticed early on and
appreciated at Auburn. By September 2018, he was promoted to director

of Academic Support Services. That promotion entailed his: (a) supervising football and volleyball academic staff; (b) serving as point of contact for both sports relating to academic eligibility; (c) providing academic and interpersonal counseling to student-athletes; and (d) serving as a liaison between athletic academic staff and the coaching staff. He even had contact with Auburn's famously successful football coach Gus Malzahn, who twice beat Alabama's football team but ultimately was driven out of his job due to booster criticism.

Thomas knew he had a challenging opportunity at Auburn but was excited about it and knew he was fully capable of handling the job. Unfortunately, another tragic blow occurred on July 8, 2019, when his dear wife of five years, Ruby, died due to breast cancer. Thomas was left with the responsibility of taking care of their 16-month-old child, Travis Jr. After his wife died, he took off one full week from work and a second week of half days, before returning the following week in full capacity.

## TRIO OF WHITE FEMALES

Thomas reported to a trio of senior associate athletic directors, all white females older than he, namely Dr. Kathryn Flynn, Cathie Helmbold, and Courtney Gage.

Thomas first came to see me on January 17, 2020, describing his unhappiness with the way this trio of white female supervisors was increasingly subjecting him to "racialized and gendered professional scrutiny and hostility," resulting in emotional distress for himself and other colleagues. As stated in paragraph 7 of his first EEOC charge of June 9, 2020, Thomas was the only male and only person of color on "the leadership team" (the other three being Flynn, Helmbold, and Gage) but was consistently "left out" of meetings and conversations privy to only these three white females. Thomas described himself as a "token to give the illusion of racial and gender progression."

With my help for six months of 2020, we pursued the diplomatic resolution with letters and telephone calls to Auburn's attorneys, also coincidentally three white females, Jaime Hammer, Moran White, and Morgan Sport. I tried to arrange a meeting with Auburn's athletic director,

Allen Greene, a Black male. But such a meeting was blocked by the three Auburn white female attorneys protecting Thomas's three white female bosses. Before his unhappiness arose, Thomas had regularly met monthly with Greene.

As Thomas further detailed in his initial EEOC charge, the nature of his work was extremely detailed and involved much strategic timing. He was on the receiving end of pressures and hostilities he considered gender connected. For example, when Thomas attempted to tell Flynn that she and the other two were overreacting to the current grades of the football team, her curt reply was "that is not something you should say to a supervisor who is also a woman."

### Inherent Culture of Fear

Thomas also described an "inherent culture of fear" among the full and part-time employees, many pressured to leave the office. Thomas's female supervisors didn't appreciate Thomas sticking up for the department's employees.

Another specific in his first charge was that, on December 18, 2019, Thomas met with Flynn to discuss how Auburn's reporting structure to the SEC was not aligned with the majority of Auburn's SEC counterparts. Thomas said Flynn directed some very hurtful and stressful comments toward him, with racial roots.

Thomas candidly acknowledged that the football players with the greatest academic challenges were African American. The Auburn administration felt that because Thomas was African American he could better handle the African American caseload. Yet Thomas said no one person is a magic wand, and no one would take the athletes' courses for them. The female supervisors shook their heads at Thomas and blamed him for the poor performance of some of the players.

Understandably, the loss of Thomas's wife, Ruby, hurt him, as did the loss of his stepson, Ruby's 10-year-old son, who he had helped raise since the age of nine months. The boy was instead sent to his biological dad. Rather than show sympathy, however, Flynn saddled Thomas with the following words, "You haven't been yourself this semester," implying that his work quality had dropped off accordingly. Flynn added, "Your ability to recall information is not as good," which caused Thomas to bring his laptop to football academic meetings after feeling he was being unduly quizzed about the students. The "coup de grace" directed at Thomas was, "The grades for the football team are the worst they've ever been," blaming him for this fact.

Accordingly, Thomas's responsibilities for supervising academic football staff were taken away and given to Thomas's immediate supervisor, white female Courtney Gage. Thus, Thomas was demoted to the job of academic counselor. He felt this unfair because the majority of his case list were "highly at-risk students," testing far lower than the average student attending Auburn University. Thomas felt the unfair blame leveled at him contained not-so-subtle racial twists.

Another unfair criticism was that Thomas needed to work on his supervisory skills. While the three white female supervisors were too smart to use racial epithets, Thomas took their criticism of his ethnic style as a put down, with gender overtones.

## EEOC Charge

Hence Thomas, in his first EEOC charge, filed on June 9, 2020, said he was being subjected to a paper trail setting him up for eventual dismissal. A copy of the charge was simultaneously sent to Auburn attorney Maran White, my favorite of the university's trio of in-house lawyers. She chastised me in a June 11, 2020, letter for not using Auburn's own in-house EEO Office. I replied in a June 15 letter that "As far as Auburn's own AA/EEO office. we have always found 100 percent of the time that it was more interested in protecting Auburn than in helping a discriminated-against employee . . ."

Unfortunately for Thomas, Auburn's treatment of him grew from bad to worse. Not happy with his first EEOC charge, cc'd to attorney White and athletic director Greene, Auburn slammed Thomas on June 30, 2020, with a much lower than ever performance review. Thomas believed this was in response to and an illegal retaliation for his June 15 EEOC charge. Hence, with my help, on July 6, 2020, Thomas filed a Supplemental

Charge of Discrimination with the EEOC, adding unlawful retaliation against him for his original complaint.

The last six months of 2020, pandemic and all, bounced along. Although Thomas wanted to reconcile and forgive, the University's feelings were not mutual. Thomas would later document exclusion from meetings and sarcastic comments toward him as very different from the way fellow white employees were treated by his three white female supervisors. Also, Flynn criticized Thomas in front of other employees ("needs work on his supervisory skills") something she rarely, if ever, did to white employees.

## THE GRADE CHANGING SCANDAL

Another issue reared its ugly head, which led to Auburn's misguided and ultimate termination of Thomas in March 2021. It involved Auburn's wrongful change of the grade of a football player, an African American graduate transfer student from Arizona State University, allowing him to play in a January 2020 bowl game, and maintain Auburn's access to the portal of graduate transfer students.

The following is what Thomas said verbatim in paragraphs 25–35 of his original lawsuit, filed on March 4, 2021, about this:

> (25) One of the many examples of the race and gender discrimination and retaliation Plaintiff Thomas was experiencing is that, in December 2019-January 2020, plaintiff (Thomas) learned that Auburn University caused, or allowed to be caused, significant pressure to be placed upon a certain female Auburn University professor to change a D (Failing grade) to a C (Passing grade) for a graduate Auburn football player, who had transferred into Auburn from Arizona State, but neglected his studies, resulting in receiving bad grades (Exhibit F). Mr. Thomas says the student was a counselee of his and that Dr. Flynn, Ms. Gage, and Ms. Helmbold, and all the coaching staff knew about the struggles of the players.

> (26) The Auburn University football team needed the grade changed not only for the graduate football player to play in Auburn's Bowl game that January 2020, but so that the Auburn football team would not lose its eligibility to accept other graduate transfers for an entire additional year.

(27)By email dated December 23, 2019, only days before the New Year's Bowl game, said professor persisted in refusing to change the football player's grade (real name of player redacted, to comply with FERPA law).

(28)Between her December 23, 2019, email, and the January 1, 2020, Bowl game said professor was caused to change her mind, or simply changed her mind, and accordingly changed the grade, thus allowing the football player to play, and further allowing Auburn University to maintain an open channel for the receipt of graduate transfer football players.

(29)Plaintiff Thomas has known about this suspicious grade change situation for at least a year (from January 2020-January 2021) and knew that his three white female supervisors (Flynn, Gage, and Helmbold) also knew that it was suspicious, and said three supervisors knew that Mr. Thomas knew about it. Plaintiff avers, on information and belief, that his knowledge of this was an additional reason why Plaintiff's three white female supervisors wanted him out of the Academic division of the Auburn University Athletic Department.

(30)At a meeting on January 28, 2021, Plaintiff felt threatened by Auburn's compliance official Rich McGlynn, when Mr. McGlynn pronounced that Mr. Thomas should have reported the possible NCAA infraction described above, even if Mr. Thomas didn't know there actually had been an infraction. Nonetheless, Mr. McGlynn also threatened that, because Auburn's rules require employees to report anything that might be a "potential violation," he, Plaintiff Thomas, could be subject to termination for failure to do so.

(31)To this threat Mr. Thomas replied that he, Plaintiff Thomas, would "only be speculating" to believe there was a potential violation, and that such "speculation" was not the same as a potential violation. Further, at a year earlier January 2020 certification meeting, the Plaintiff had brought this entire matter up to the Leadership Team, the Auburn Compliance Office, the Faculty Athletic representative, and the Registrar's office, so everyone knew about what was going on an entire year earlier. Thus, no one could correctly say Mr. Thomas was hiding information.

(32)After this email from Professor Nelson, Mr. Thomas was not informed of any activities concerning the student after that, until the

January 2020 certification meeting. Present at that certification meeting were the Register's office, Athletics Compliance office, Faculty Athletic Representative, Senior Athletic Director for SASS, two Associate Athletic Directors for SASS, Director of Academic Support Services and Football Academic Counselors. During that meeting Mr. Thomas brought up that this student should have been ineligible because he did not receive two C's to play in the bowl game, or to remain eligible for Spring 2020. Mr. Thomas raised concerns at that meeting but was informed "you know his grade got changed." The conversations were awkward, but Mr. Thomas never received any information on the grade change until that meeting. Further when Mr. Thomas brought up the grade change in the meeting, it was laughed off by people present, as if it was no big deal.

(33) Mr. Thomas himself did not actually know about the grade change until after the meeting, although it apparently came a couple of days after the original email from the professor saying she would not change the grade. Mr. Thomas was never informed of the grade change, which broke Auburn's normal operating procedures. Anytime a grade change normally came through it was forwarded, at the very latest, to Mr. Thomas on the day of the change, not weeks later.

(34) Plaintiff Thomas's knowledge of the matters described above was, and/or is, another reason why all three of his white female supervisors, and defendant Auburn University itself, wanted Plaintiff terminated, or otherwise pressured to leave.

(35) Plaintiff's three white female supervisors all knew about the professor's apparently pressured grade change, which made possible the Auburn football player's eligibility for the January 1, 2020 bowl game, yet none of said three white females were ever threatened about their knowledge, nor were they ever threatened with termination, despite their failure to report it to Auburn University itself, just as Auburn has been accusing the Plaintiff of doing in its notice of termination.

(36) The more gentle and respectful way the three white females were treated by Auburn University, as compared to the more antagonistic and disrespectful way Plaintiff himself, a young black male, was blamed, constituted race and sex discrimination against the Plaintiff himself.

## PRESS REACTION

Once the lawsuit was filed, the press was all over it, saying that Auburn University had some serious questions to answer.

Sportswriter Tom Green of AL.com headlined a front-page story in the *Birmingham News* with the words: "Allegation of Grade Changing at Auburn Comes to Light." He added that former Auburn tight end/H-back Jay Jay Wilson is the only player from 2019 who fit that description. Mike Eads of the *Opelika-Auburn Daily News* ran a strong article challenging Auburn to respond. Kathy Lohr of National Public Radio ran a story titled "Auburn Prepares for Post-Scandal Football." ESPN writer Carly McClure reprinted a story about another Auburn football cheater crisis three years earlier, implying that Thomas's case was more of the same.

*Birmingham News* (and AL.com) sports columnist Joseph Goodman's opening phrase in a five-page online and hard copy story read: "The living hell that Travis Thomas has endured over the past few years is almost too much to process. The nightmare started when his 32-year-old wife was diagnosed with breast cancer. It killed Ruby Thomas in six months, leaving Thomas with a toddler to raise alone."

In response to Thomas's race discrimination claim, Goodman added: "As for Auburn's whiteness, it is indeed the whitest school in the SEC, according to U.S. News 2019 campus ethnic diversity rating system. Auburn scored a 0.27, with 1.0 being the highest possible score for diversity. That puts Auburn right there with BYU and the University of Charleston. I would argue that Ole Miss and Alabama historically have a whiter "criticized image" than Auburn, but that's not really a debate anyone wins."

## AUBURN PROFESSOR KATHRYN NELSON

Auburn Professor Kathryn Nelson's email of Monday, December 23, 2019, at 8:15 a.m. precisely read:

> To:Jay Jay Wilson
> Cc:James White
> Good Morning, Jay Jay
> After consideration of your performance and final grade in ADED

7626, and after having discussed this situation with the Interim Chair of the LEFT department, I am sending this to inform you that your final grade will remain as is. If you have any further questions about this matter, you may reach out to me via email.)

Thank you.

Kate Nelson, PhD.

Adjunct Professor—Education Foundation Leadership, and Technology Instructor—First Year Seminar

After the lawsuit was filed, Auburn's exceedingly competent outside attorneys Dorman Walker and Aria Allen were quick to file motions to dismiss, raising everything but the kitchen sink, to use a colloquial phrase.

Federal Judge Austin Huffaker, attempting to carefully review our complaint and hold us to a high standard of precision, twice made telephone calls to me and my law partner, co-counsel David Sawyer of Birmingham, suggesting what he needed to make the complaint tighter. In hindsight, we appreciated it.

With David leading the heavy lifting of revisions, and working with Thomas and me, we filed a First Amended Complaint on April 9, 2021, and a Second Amended Complaint on June 30, 2021, clarifying certain issues.

## JUDGE HUFFAKER'S OPINION

A seven-month extended period passed from July 1, 2021, until February 11, 2022, before federal Judge Huffaker issued a very favorable 19-page Memorandum Opinion and Order, denying defendant Auburn University's motion to dismiss. His order thus opened discovery and depositions. I regret that it took 11 months to get such a ruling, but Judge Huffaker's more notable comments included the following:

This discriminatorily hostile environment (at the Auburn University athletic department) was not unique to him as other black employees felt the same. Because of the treatment toward black employees, Thomas claims there was frequent employee turnover, pointing to two black employees who were pressured to leave the athletics department. According to Thomas, white employees seemed to fare better than their black counterparts because hurtful and disparaging comments were hurled at black employees but not white employees.

As to the grade changing scandal and termination, Judge Huffaker added:

> In December 2019, a grade-changing scandal developed within the Auburn athletic department. A football player was failing a class and needed a passing grade in order to play in an upcoming bowl game. According to Thomas, Auburn officials wanted the player's professor to switch the player's grade from failing to passing, but the professor refused to do so. (Doc 28 at 15)
>
> Concerned about the pressure being applied to the professor to make the grade change, in January 2020, Thomas brought this matter to the attention of the academic leadership team including Flynn, Gage, and Helmbold; the Auburn compliance office; the faculty athletic representative; and the registrar's office . . . that concern apparently fell upon deaf ears because during a certification meeting several weeks later, Thomas was told that the player's "grade got changed" . . .
>
> A year later, however, Auburn officials turned the issue against Thomas. During a meeting on January 28, 2021, and contrary to what Thomas actually had done a year earlier, Auburn's compliance officer told Thomas that he should have reported the grade changing incident because not doing so was an NCAA infraction . . .
>
> A month later, on March 1, 2021, Auburn fired Thomas . . . Thomas alleges that Flynn, Gage, Helmbold all knew about the grade changing scandal and failed to report it to compliance officials, but unlike him, they were not threatened or fired . . .

Thus, the battle was joined, and frankly, based on the above, it was hard to believe the Auburn University's Athletics Department was acting in good faith. In June 2022, I took depositions of Athletic Director Allen

Greene, Professor Kathryn Nelson, and Athletic Department Supervisor Kathryn Flynn. Assisting me in the deposition as an expert witness was newly retained professor Derryn Moten of Alabama State University, chairman of his school's history and civil rights department. Auburn also took the deposition of Thomas.

On September 21, 2022, I took the deposition of compliance official Rich McGlynn, by then the acting athletic director, replacing Allen Greene, whose departure weeks earlier was attributed in the media to unhappiness on both sides, Auburn's and Greene's.

In the summer of 2022, we were also contacted by an official of the NCAA in Indianapolis. We answered that Travis Thomas was wrongfully terminated by Auburn as a scapegoat for its own wrongdoing, and for not reporting information concerning the suspicious grade change, which information Thomas did not have. What Thomas did know was way less than what his three female supervisors knew. On September 26, 2022, I returned to Auburn to take the deposition of Dr. Jim Witte, department head of the grade-changing professor, Nelson.

We learned from McGlynn and Witte that Auburn University knowingly engaged in a grade-changing, we believe improper under NCAA rules, using as an excuse that the student involved (initials JJW) was given a passing C grade, based on an untruth that the student's sister had actually committed suicide. Professor Nelson had three times previously refused to change the grade based on an "attempted suicide" excuse. But one day after Christmas 2019, Henderson was led by Witte, her department head, into believing the untruth. And Witte confirmed that he had spoken with Flowers, the dean of the Auburn University College of Arts and Science, and Hargrave, the provost, before passing on the misinformation about the football player's sister to Nelson, causing her to change the football player's grade.

So, who's the bully in this case? Let you, the reader, determine. This story is far from over.

# 19

# University Women Vigilant

The cases of the following four women hammer home my point that despite its wise attorneys, Auburn University stumbles in its mistreatment of employees. It sometimes clearly amounts to bullying. The permission of each to share the non-confidential aspects of their stories, pulled from their EEOC charges, public records, has been given to me. I refer to: (a) Robbi Beauchamp and (b) Heather Gideon, both of Auburn University's College of Veterinary Medicine until their dismissal in March 2022. I also refer to (c) Jennifer Wells-Marshall, College of Human Sciences; and (d) Gail Butcher, both formerly of Auburn University's Office of Research. Both were dismissed in 2021.

## ROBBI BEAUCHAMP

The first to see me was Robbi Beauchamp on March 26, 2021. A 59-year-old white female, she was a long-time Auburn employee. In 1985, she started as Vice President of Business and Finance in the Office of the Comptroller. By March 2013, she had moved to the College of Veterinary Medicine (CVM) at Auburn University. She began as an administrative assistant and fundraiser. Her employee ratings were always the highest.

Beauchamp reluctantly reported that, in the four years preceding her March 2021 termination, she often observed strong evidence of age discrimination. Increasingly younger employees were being hired at pay ranges higher than entry-level. They had only limited past experience in higher education. Meanwhile, older employees were terminated or forced out on pretextual grounds. The bogus charge against her was that she had falsified time sheets. Beauchamp was one of three mid-fifties females. Heather Gideon and Jerri Turnbough, the others, were wrongfully terminated by the Veterinary Medicine School in March 2021. Beauchamp also quoted a newer much younger admissions coordinator, Tijuan Sellars, above her in rank. She openly made comments, where management could hear, that older employees were "unwilling to change." They were also "set in their ways" and "needed to go."

Beauchamp was denied a pre-termination hearing and a post-termination hearing. This gave rise to a violation of due process claims against Auburn University.

The same Sellars, a young African American male, was observed by Beauchamp making racially charged comments. One was "I don't want to be called African American." Another was "I don't like to use honorifics," such as Mr. (Mister) and Mrs. (Mistress), "because they are rooted in slavery." Beauchamp observed that older white female identities of herself and Gideon made Sellars uncomfortable. Beauchamp also had reliable information that Sellars was the driving force behind the dismissal of Gideon and her with false accusations.

Beauchamp amicably tried to settle and resolve her differences with Auburn several times before litigation. Yet Auburn continually stonewalled her. She felt forced to file suit on August 19, 2022.

## HEATHER GIDEON

Heather Gideon came to see me a month later, on April 19, 2021, also wrongfully terminated. The College of Veterinary Medicine (CVM) reinforced what Beauchamp said. A 53-year-old white female, she had a sterling record that included a master's degree at Westminster Presbyterian Seminary in California. There she also served as admissions director, financial aid coordinator, registrar, and dean of Women's Studies.

Gideon's background was of great value and assistance to the CVM when hired in 2014. At its Office of Academic Affairs, Gideon provided invaluable assistance. She produced numerous reports and provided support for clinical software. She also did exam proctoring and contacted outside agencies regarding student needs. Gideon also performed many other responsibilities.

Gideon noticed that during the preceding five years many younger people came to the CVM at pay ranges higher than normal entry-level.

Gideon said in paragraph 7 of her EEOC Charge: "From 2017–2021, comments have been openly made in front of management by Admissions Coordinator Tijuan Sellars and others that "older employees were unwilling to change and needed to go." He added that "younger people were more in tune with what needed to be done, while older people were "set in their ways" and "unwilling to change." She added that younger staff members "routinely ignored, did not communicate with, and openly treated older staff members with contempt. This was never corrected by senior management such as Givens, associate dean of academic affairs."

Gideon described in paragraphs 9–13 of her EEOC charge the pretextual grounds upon which she was terminated.

(9) On March 4, 2021, I was in the common area of the Office of Academic Affairs of the College of Veterinary Medicine at the workstation of Ms. Jerri Turnbough. The reason I was there was to let Ms. Turnbough know that the meeting I had been in was finished, and I could now resume proctoring students taking exams. I did not know that the student with the accommodation we were proctoring had already finished her exam.

(10) At that same time, I did not notice that a video was being shown on Ms. Turnbough's workstation. I was not there for that purpose, initially paid it no attention, and was oblivious to its being shown. As Ms. Turnbough and I discussed the exam proctoring, I noted the video showing the students who were still sitting in the testing rooms and a conference room was forbidden to be seen, and I learned absolutely nothing from what was displayed.

(11) I was therefore flabbergasted when I learned the next day that because I had allegedly "watched" the video depicting a meeting taking place, I was being placed on administrative leave.

(12) Twelve days later, on March 17, 2021, I received a notice from the HR manager of the College of Veterinary Medicine that I was being terminated due to having "watched" the video. I was shocked, devastated, and overwhelmed, especially because I never "watched" the video, even though I was aware that it was being shown. I paid little attention to the video and didn't know the subject matter of the meeting the video was depicting.

(13) In my case, I was falsely accused of "having watched a confidential meeting," though the specific date, time, and participants of the meeting were never specified by a representative of the College of Veterinary Medicine. Any portion of any meeting I happened to see the week of March 1, 2021, occurred in the routine performance of my duties.

Gideon could not believe how she had been railroaded and "shanghaied," so to speak. After being wrongfully terminated, she took advantage of steps provided by Auburn to reach a resolution. That included meeting with the dean of the CVM. She pursued a grievance hearing on June 23, 2021. She also learned for the first time that her termination was based on statements provided by an unidentified "witness" (Sellars). She made statements in good faith at a surprise "fact-finding" meeting, which became a pre-termination hearing.

Gideon saw me on multiple occasions, accompanied by an associate dean of another college at Auburn University. His name will remain undisclosed. He believed Gideon was terribly wronged.

Gideon was stonewalled by Auburn in her multiple efforts to resolve and settle her case. As a result, she filed suit in April 2022.

## Dr. Jennifer Wells-Marshall

On May 10, 2021, I met Dr. Jennifer Wells-Marshall, a 47-year-old female of African American descent. I was captivated by her charm and humble manner.

Wells-Marshall had long been at Auburn. She had two higher education degrees there. The first, in 2005, was an MS in Human Development and Family Studies. She concentrated on Child Development and Family Relations.

Wells-Marshall's second Auburn degree, a doctorate, was in Educational Psychology. Her dissertation was on a development model for Auburn's Cooperative Extension Program.

Auburn's bad history on race relations was reflected by its low rating as the "whitest school in the SEC" (see the *U.S. News* 2019 campus ethnic diversity rating as reported by *Birmingham News* sports columnist in March 2021). The Auburn University Extension Service ("ACES") and Auburn's College of Human Services (CHS) have long been closely connected with many interdepartmental courses. ACES long had a much friendlier relationship with its Caucasian employees than its African American employees. ACES' leadership had been dominated for years by four older white men (see Chapter 5). Historically in Alabama, there have been two "Extension Service" schools, the one in Huntsville, at Alabama A&M University, historically Black; the other at Auburn University, the white school.

By 2019, Wells-Marshall had become the executive director and clinical professor in the Family Childcare Partnership. She worked directly with Head Start programs statewide. This sounded like an Extension Service program, housed in CHS. Her supervision of managers and directors included 37 direct reports, 43 contractor reports, and 160 network members. Her job description called for her to develop and implement outreach initiatives, secure funding, and build partnerships to expand public services.

Wells-Marshall was the dynamic perfect person for the job. She enjoyed great support among her staff as outreach administrators.

She came to see me that March 2021, stating she was "under pressure." She was wrongfully non-renewed in her job. She said she wasn't sure about anything else. However, she was "100 percent sure her non-renewal was due to her race."

In the near lily-white fields of Auburn, Wells-Marshall was the first African American administrator in the College of Human Science. She unfortunately was treated disrespectfully by the one person above her in rank, Dr. Angela Wiley, a Caucasian.

I immediately helped Wells-Marshall prepare a charge of race discrimination with the Equal Employment Opportunity Commission (EEOC) on April 22, 2021. Seven months later, on November 29, 2021, a right-to-sue letter was recovered from the EEOC.

Law partner David Sawyer and I carefully crafted a suit. We polished several revisions before filing it on February 22, 2022. Wells-Marshall described how Black employees at ACES received written reprimands and terminations at Auburn for the same policy infraction as whites who were not reprimanded or terminated.

During a telephone call in June 2020, Christal Coker, a Caucasian subordinate and family and community engagement specialist, verbally swore at Wells-Marshall in front of eight subordinate employees, all white. This fully undermined Wells-Marshall's authority.

Wells-Marshall sought assistance from the Colleges' HR director and obtained statements about Coker's belligerency. That director said, "I can't do anything until I talk with Angela Wiley." Most unfortunately, Wiley refused to help, undercutting Wells-Marshall's leadership as executive director.

Our client criticized the double standard write-ups for Blacks. Nothing was done against white employees engaged in similar or worse behavior. Wells-Marshall, in a comprehensive "Statement of Facts," 84 paragraphs in length, cited many incidents of disparity. There was an enormous communication gap with Wiley.

Rather than meet directly with Wells-Marshall to reconcile or better communicate, Wiley sent her a letter on October 22, 2022. She terminated her as Executive Director, effective May 30, 2021.

In our lawsuit, neither Auburn University nor Wiley offered any reason for Wells-Marshall's termination. If they had, it would have been a pretext for race discrimination.

Auburn filed a motion to dismiss. Wells-Marshall, without anyone's assistance, responded with a strong defense of our case. When this book went to publication, the motion was still pending, with no ruling.

## GAIL BUTCHER

Gail Butcher was the last of the four above-named women coming to see me about Auburn University. We met on January 7, 2022, as I listened to her carefully. Previously employed by Auburn for 28 years, she had a legitimate basis for her disgruntlement. She worked at Auburn's Office of Research Compliance for the preceding 13 years, 10 of which were comfortable under her supervisor Roger Bridgeman. The job was a "second home and family" for her, as she strived to treat her fellow employees well.

Unfortunately, Butcher's last three years (2019–2022) were under a new supervisor, Sally Headley, who continually subjected Butcher to verbal abuse and insults. According to paragraph 4 of Butcher's Equal Employment Opportunity Commission (EEOC) charge, Headley went further, kicking walls and copy machines and slamming doors. She also raised her voice at employees. She even demeaned Butcher's grandchild as "the fat kid," etc.

Headley was close to Butcher. She easily saw how she suffered from anxiety and depression in recent years. Despite its sensitivity, Headley allowed this disability to fuel her increasingly abusive behavior toward Butcher. That included efforts to get rid of Butcher.

As Butcher soldiered on, attempting to be objective, with a constructive voice for Auburn's Office of Research Compliance, Headley continued to degrade her.

By January 19, 2022, the situation had become bad enough I assisted Butcher in filing, with my assistance, "a disability discrimination" complaint with the (EEOC) in Birmingham. She complained about "egregiously unprofessional behavior" swept under the rug and ignored. She added that Headley's outbursts and grossly offensive language "escalated her anxiety and depression."

Butcher added, "the pressure became so severe, pervasive, and even perverse that I could not continue to endure it any longer. Instead, she resigned under pressure, to protect her sanity, in what I now understand can legally be called a 'constructive discharge.'"

In suffering the "constructive discharge," amounting to a termination, Butcher affirmed she had been discriminated against, due to her disability. This was in violation of the Americans with Disabilities Act, Amendments Act of 2008 (ADAAA) (42 U.S.C. § 12101, et seq.)

Butcher received a right-to-sue from the EEOC on August 18, 2022. A day later, declaring she was worn out from fighting the battle, Butcher decided not to file suit.

## 20

# Summary Judgment Bullies

This is not sexy. Please understand this important development has undermined an important protection of life. I refer to summary judgment bullies.

When I first broke into active law practice in Alabama in the mid-1970s, the "scintilla rule" was the standard for summary judgment in civil litigation cases. That meant, so long as there is a small piece of evidence, judges could not dismiss a plaintiff's case on a summary judgment motion filed by the defense. That law has drastically changed. An enormous abuse of summary judgment has grown like kudzu since the late 1980s. It has given judges, especially in civil rights and employment cases, a stranglehold that truly bullies.

In earlier years, the little guy had a decent shot against powerhouse corporate entities, who could stand up to bullies. Some judges stomp on victims, especially in the federal arena, whether they realize it or not.

Somewhere, somehow, powerful corporate interests lost too many cases. They didn't like paying for misconduct, despite hurting people. Despite their far superior resources, they got organized politically. They also got legislation passed in 1987 to increase the standard to a higher "substantial evidence" rule. This has dramatically altered the legal landscape.

The Code of Alabama, section 12–21-12, was amended as follows:

(a) In all civil actions brought in many courts of the State of Alabama, proof by substantial evidence shall be required to submit an issue of fact to the trier of facts; (b) The scintilla rule of evidence is hereby abolished in all civil actions in the courts of the State of Alabama."

To judges, this meant a plaintiff had to produce strong evidence to avoid being thrown out of court. The Code of Alabama added:

> Substantial evidence shall mean evidence of such quality and weight that reasonable and fair-minded persons, in the exercise of impartial judgment, might reach different conclusions as to the existence of facts sought to be proven.

The federal courts of Alabama soon adopted this same ultra-high standard in Celotex Corp. v. Catrett, 477 U.S. 317 (1986); Anderson v. Liberty Lobby, 477 U.S. 242 (1986); and Matsushita Electric Industrial Co. v. Zenith Radio Corp., 475 U.S. 574 (1986).

On the surface, this was a bad idea. Unfortunately, judges often abuse the standard, causing a gross injustice to people of modest means.

The origins of the summary judgment law were quite different. With its roots in English common law, it was in 1938 that the summary judgment motion became codified in America. It began with Rule 56 of the Federal Rules of Civil Procedure. At first, it was infrequently used. As recently as 1975, the 2nd Circuit U.S. Court of Appeals remarked that "summary judgment" was a drastic device. Its prophylactic function, when exercised, cuts off a party's right to present its case to the jury. Heyman v. Commerce & Indus Ins. Co., 524 F.2d 1317,1320 (2nd Cir. 1975).

Regrettably to parties seeking civil justice, this new standard choked off many worthy causes. Because the "substantial evidence" standard is so subjective, it runs the gamut from one to 1,000. The philosophies or politics of judges differ considerably.

In Alabama, bully companies like Alfa Corporation dominate politics. Alfa gives $100,000 to each state senate candidate and $50,000 to each state representative candidate it supports. See Steve Flowers's column in the *Montgomery Independent* of August 9, 2018.

Alfa will put much into campaigns through its political arm, the Alabama Farmers Federation. It puts much more into the state-wide campaigns of U.S. Senate candidates it favors. Alfa is highly motivated to influence judicial appointments. That includes U.S. magistrate judges. They often aspire to a full U.S. district court seat. In fact, the court always favors attorneys from established law firms.

Historically U.S. presidents pick federal judges. The White House generally defers to the recommendations of U.S. senators from states. It then nominates someone for an available opening. This happens even when you have Democratic presidents like Barack Obama and Joe Biden. Nonetheless Alabama's Republican U.S. Senators, (Jeff Sessions or Richard Shelby), can easily block the judicial nomination process. Alfa and Alabama Power Company can easily pick their candidates for a judgeship. They can veto candidates they don't like. This happens as in a state like Alabama.

The "little guy's" socio-economic interests are more aligned with Democratic presidents. He frequently gets slapped or popped in the head by judges, sympathetic to interests who want them nominated.

The last time the Middle District of Alabama had a judge sympathetic to the little-guy was Judge Myron Thompson. He was nominated by President Jimmy Carter to a federal judgeship in 1979. Thompson is an enormous hero to me, a jurist unafraid to stand up to powerful corporate and governmental interests. How I wish we had more judges like Thompson. He is 10 years past the voluntary retirement age of 65, and only six months younger than me. He turned 75 in 2022. He is not likely to be on the federal bench much longer, although he is currently in good health.

All three recent federal judicial appointments for the Middle District of Alabama come from Montgomery's establishment law firms, namely Rushton, Stakely, Johnston, & Garrett (Judge Austin Huffaker); Ball, Ball, Duke, and Matthews (Judge Emily Marks); Capell, Howard, Knabe, & Cobbs (Judge Jerusha Adams); and Balch and Bingham (Judge Kelly Pate). These are all great law firms. All the lawyers elevated to judgeships are women and men of integrity and intellect. But they came from heavily corporate firms dedicated to maintaining the status quo. The personal philosophy of the judge, if only subconsciously, makes great differences in decision-making.

U.S. Magistrate Judge Stephen Doyle informed me and others at a mediation a year ago that 60 percent of summary judgment motions result in rulings for defendants. Meanwhile, 60 percent of plaintiff's cases get thrown out before arriving at a courtroom. I cited that figure to defense attorney Dorman Walker of Balch and Bingham. He was surprised it was that low.

In my last book, *Only in Alabama*, I explained in 19 how "Alfa the Bully" had wrongfully fired Jennifer Akridge. It was definitely the result of expensive medical treatment for multiple sclerosis. The enormous Alfa political influence worked against her. This was despite overwhelming evidence that Akridge's multiple sclerosis disability was the true reason for her termination.

Fortunately, the higher Eleventh Circuit Court of Appeals rescued us in Akridge v. Alfa Mut. Ins. Co., 1 F.4th 1271 (11th Cir. 2021), reversing Magistrate Judge Gray Borden for not allowing us to take a key deposition of a top human resources official of Alfa. The appellate court sent it back to the district court for further disposition. Surprisingly, albeit with a new judge whose identity will remain undisclosed, we experienced summary judgment again. We were back in the Eleventh Circuit at the time this was written.

In my book, *Only in Alabama*, I set forth case law and guiding legal standards. If followed, they would easily have enabled us to defeat "Alfa the Bully," and other similar corporate bullies.

## SUMMARY JUDGMENT STANDARD

Here's what the law on summary judgment says. Rule 56(a) of the Federal Rules of Civil Procedure (FRCP) allows summary judgment only "if the movant shows that no genuine dispute exists, as to any material fact." A judge must follow this case law precedent . . . A court must draw all reasonable inferences in favor of the nonmoving party. Standard v. A.B.E.L. Servs., Inc., 161 F.3d 1318, 1326 (11th Cir. 1998).

The trial court's function . . . is not to weigh the evidence, it must determine the truth of the matter. It must simply determine whether a genuine issue exists for trial." Anderson v. Liberty Lobby, Inc., 477 U.S. 242, 249–50, 106 S. Ct. 2505, 91 L. Ed. 2d 202 (1986). By these legal standards, plaintiffs should more easily get past the summary judgment hurdle.

Further, the guiding standard of the Eleventh Circuit Court of Appeals is that a lower court must avoid weighing the evidence, and it must also make credibility determinations of the truth of the matter. Instead, the evidence of the non-moving party must be believed. Then all justifiable inferences must be drawn in his or her favor. Tipton v. Bergrohr GMBH-Siegen, 965 F.2d 994, 999 (11th Cir. 1992). Unfortunately, this standard has been ignored by many courts.

Our Akridge appellate brief stated that, according to all legal precedents, summary judgment against Akridge should have been denied. We also cited the Eleventh Circuit case of Beard v. Annis, 730 F.2d 741, 743 (1984). It held that, in employment cases, involving as they do, "nebulous questions of motivation and intent," summary judgment is inappropriate for resolving such claims.

It was not like Alfa didn't know about Akridge's disability and its related costs that were staring them in the face. The record was replete with evidence that all Alfa managers ranking above Akridge knew about her multiple sclerosis disability. No other plausible, rational, or logical explanation existed or could be credibly shown. Her termination maintained her costly disability. Alfa even ignored that Akridge helped save Alfa $2 million in her last year. This was a clear-cut violation of the Americans with Disabilities Act.

Alfa was openly sensitive about saving medical costs, due to its using self-insurance. Evidence also existed that Alfa warned its employees to be careful about such costs. The smoking gun came in August 2017. At that point Akridge's COBRA medication extension was cancelled, eight months after her termination by Alfa. This was though she was still covered by her original policy.

More favorable evidence for Akridge existed in that a "comparator" person in Akridge's underwriting department, Hillary McCaleb, was equally affected by the same automation. It was also used as an excuse for terminating Akridge. Yet Alfa moved McCaleb to another job. It also did this to several other underwriting department employees. None of the others cost Alfa any money for disability treatment. Akridge's superiors said during depositions that Akridge's responsibilities were not eliminated by automation. Why was Akridge removed?

Overwhelming evidence existed that Akridge's disability was the only reason she was involuntarily terminated. It was a significant and motivating factor, and the only plausible reason for defeating summary judgment. This re-emphasizes my point that increasingly high standards for granting summary judgment have bullied plaintiffs.

This is the type of client our law firm represents!

For the sake of courtesy, and out of respect for the judiciary, I will refrain from calling the names, or genders, of any federal judge to whose cases I have been referring. A reasonable sleuth might uncover identities. Judiciaries in the U.S. District Courts of Mobile and Montgomery, are known for being pro-establishment in employment discrimination cases.

I remember leading Mobile employment attorney Henry Brewster telling me that a "$20,000 settlement" was "good money in Mobile." Recently our firm had two federal cases from the Selma division of Mobile's Southern District Court, which defeated summary judgment. One involved Ronita Wade against Dario Melton, the mayor of Selma, ultimately worth $250,000, and not subject to confidentiality. The other involved a $95,000 settlement, not subject to confidentiality, but that client's name will not be mentioned here. In both cases, one involved Judge Kristi DuBose and the other involved Judge Jeffrey Beaverstock. Both judges denied summary judgment, allowing us to have a jury trial. I respect and appreciate both judges, who protected both clients from being bullied.

Another federal judge in Montgomery has aggrieved me greatly with three prematurely negative summary judgment rulings that unfairly bully people. Their stories, shared with their permission and encouragement in this book, involve Marie Carastro, in her late 80s; Marshall Burns, in his mid-70s; and David Sanchez, in his mid-50s. All three cases had strong age discrimination details. All facts in their favor were overlooked by the court.

The shame in all three cases is that average jurors could easily have found multiple "genuine issues for trial," and easily could have ruled in favor of Carastro, Burns, and Sanchez. The Court's granting of summary judgment in favor of three corporate defendants bullied all these plaintiffs.

Age discrimination is not "rattled" in one's face, like race or sex cases are. Age discrimination is "never shouted from the rooftops," using a phrase I employ in opening or closing argument. Age discrimination is more insidious, lurking beneath the surface, very painful.

Age discrimination slapped Mike Keller in the face, a star performer as a 50-year-old gifted employee at Hyundai. In 2018, the corporation decided to rid itself of 21 highly competent and productive employees. Their salaries were terminated (see Chapter 8). All let go were over 40, and the majority over 50. Thank God, we drew the fearless and brilliant Myron Thompson as our judge. He compared Hyundai to "Wile E. Coyote," denying summary judgment to that corporation.

I've seen deep depression in the faces of men and women in their 40s, 50s, and 60s. Suddenly replaced by someone in his or her 30s, who was much less competent. This happens way too often. It's not hard to spot. Age discrimination exists, pure and simple, no matter how much an employer may disguise it, or how much a pro-establishment judge may spin it. This is what the U.S. Congress tried to stop. There are too many courts that overlook and allow this to happen.

## MARIE CARASTRO

Marie Carastro was "Ninety Years Old and Still Truckin'" stated the title of chapter 7 of my book, *Only in Alabama*.

An invaluable employee for many years of the Alabama Department of Public Health, Carastro was an expert in the field of food safety, as an inspector of nursing homes and independent facilities across the state. She had a messianic sense of duty, even legendary. Occasionally it was "a burr in the saddle" for facilities less enthralled about her high safety standards. To counter, unhappy bureaucrats diminished her personality traits and falsely accused her of "premature dementia."

By the time we got to court, we filed four charges of age discrimination with the Equal Employment Opportunity Commission (EEOC) in Birmingham, laden with strong facts in her favor, and she received rights-to-sue on each.

The evidence of age discrimination against Carastro was overwhelming. It was really undeniable. Her amazing energy and enthusiasm sometimes blew me away. She finally retired at 89, with her lawsuit pending.

At her 90th birthday party that I attended on March 28, 2019, Carastro received certificates of commendation from both Governor Kay Ivey and U.S. Congresswoman Terri Sewell.

This should have been a "no way to lose" case of age discrimination. We had many sworn witnesses and deposition excerpts, supporting Carastro. Thus, we were all shocked when a federal judge granted summary judgment against Carastro. Maybe this younger judge considered Carastro's high 80s age as "too old to work." It was a huge miscarriage of justice, given the great job Carastro did. It had a bullying effect.

## MARSHALL BURNS

Dr. Marshall Burns was only one-year older than me at 73, when he first came to see us on November 5, 2018. His textbooks had been used for years by colleges and universities throughout America, including at the prestigious Stanford University in California. While lobbying for more funding at the Alabama Legislature, Tuskegee University's administration waved Burns's textbook at legislators as a proud example of Tuskegee's astute scholarship. He had been voted "Teacher of the Year" by Tuskegee students from a panel chosen by other Tuskegee professors and the University's president as well.

Unbelievably, in 2018, after 42 years of professorship, Burns was only making $60,500 annually. Meanwhile younger full professors, virtually all of different races or national origins than native-born Caucasian Americans were being paid $70,000 to $90,000. We also raised a national origin claim in his case. Regrettably, Burns's salary hadn't been raised during the prior 12 years. Nonetheless his younger Asian colleagues were galloping upwards financially.

Even more amazing was that Tuskegee University had a handbook for faculty listing race, sex, national origin, religion, and disability as demographics protected against discrimination. Conspicuously missing was any prohibition against age discrimination. Our judge ignored this omission and agreed with the University that it was only a typographical error. However, it wasn't, because it was repeated in at least two handbooks, one updating the other.

The entire case seemed like a "slam dunk" to me. Instead, on a summary judgment motion filed by defendant Tuskegee University, this same judge "slam dunked" my client and me.

To say that Burns and I were knocked, shocked, bruised, and contused, to use a poetical phrase, is a vast understatement. I wondered if that particular judge had a grudge against me personally. That same judge, 10 to 12 years earlier, as a private practice attorney, filed a Bar complaint against me because I used the word "embellish" in describing certain witnesses of hers in a lawyer's unemployment compensation case. The Alabama State Bar's disciplinary arm quickly rejected the complaint as frivolous and didn't even ask me to reply. A judge's "personal peeves," human as they are, sometimes generate a "subconscious bias." I was hoping this was not the case, yet I was beginning to wonder.

Back to the esteemed professor and national textbook-writer, Dr. Marshall Burns . . . he was so fed up with the judicial process and disheartened, and so worn out at 75, that he decided not to appeal despite my offer to help him do so.

## David Sanchez

The youngest of my three age discrimination cases with this judge involved Dr. David Sanchez. He was only 54 years old when he first came to see me on December 8, 2017. Age 54 is fairly far along in the age employment spectrum. A licensed physical therapist since 1997, he was working for the U.S. Air Force through MEDS, a civilian medical contactor. Ironically, Sanchez had developed orthopedic issues of his own. That included spine pain and arthritis in his arms and legs.

Unfortunately for Sanchez, a muscular 32-year-old female triathlon star became his supervisor. She started making cynical and ageist remarks about David and his disability. This included calling Sanchez "a scatterbrain." She even shook her fist at Sanchez to intimidate him. Another more senior Maxwell officer commented to Sanchez that "you and I must be out of touch with new concepts." This referred to the triathlon star's younger age and training.

This time I was not surprised when the same judge issued a third summary judgment. He dismissed Sanchez's case on the defendants' summary judgment motion. Sanchez authorized us to appeal his case to the Eleventh Circuit Court of Appeals. That we did, where the case was amicably resolved. Read between the lines on that comment!

I am not challenging the ethics or the character of judges. That includes this judge, on the federal or state judiciary levels of Alabama. When summary judgment motions are granted against less powerful plaintiffs, it simply is judicial philosophy, always hard to challenge. The standards for summary judgment are in bad need of substantial revamping to protect civil rights and the Fourteenth Amendment's Constitutional due process protections of American citizens. I might add the Sixth Amendment U.S. Constitutional right to confront one's accuser, with a trial by jury, is in need of protection.

Enough said. Someone, please help! . . . Be ye legislator, judge, chief executive, or whoever, please listen, and help the plaintiffs' bar stand up to these bullies.

## 21

# Immunity Defense Kills Civil Rights

In 2021, we had three major injury cases come to the McPhillips Shinbaum law firm from victims of law enforcement brutality. Two involved wrongful deaths, and the third rendered a client paraplegic. Talk about being bullied; it doesn't get much worse than that.

One case involved a deputy sheriff of Elmore County shooting and killing a 32-year-old decorated veteran of the Afghan war, Jonathan Pears. Also wounded was his 60-year-old father, Andrew Pears, a retired U.S. Air Force colonel and veteran of Afghanistan, Iraq, and Desert Storm. This happened on July 27, 2021, only four days after young Jonathan had escorted his mother to her seat at his sister's wedding.

A second case involved an October 17, 2021, shooting in the back of Tidera Harris by a City of Montgomery police officer. This happened after the officer first checked Harris's identity, saw no weapons, and charged Harris with no crime. Our client was only walking away. For months, the City of Montgomery stonewalled us, refusing to turn over bodycam video footage. When they finally did, it became the subject of a protective order. No one could see the video but us. No wonder. The footage was damning . . . it was a "George Floyd" type of police brutality that rendered Harris paraplegic.

The third case involved a killing at the Bullock Correctional Facility near Union Springs, Alabama. There a pack of mentally deranged inmates bludgeoned another inmate, Larry Brown, to death, while a single female correctional officer on duty, fairly new on the job, stood by afraid to prevent it out of fear for her own life. The two wardens knew about this woeful absence of security, as did state prison commissioner Jefferson Dunn. We have alleged the wardens and Dunn wantonly and intentionally failed to provide adequate protection for inmates.

Accordingly, we filed lawsuits against defendants in all three cases. Primarily assisted by law partner David Sawyer, and secondarily by associate attorney Andrea Hatchcock, the team also included semi-retired former partner Kenneth Shinbaum, paralegal Cesaire Jane McPherson, and office manager Amy Strickland. Amy prepared the paperwork in both the Pears and Brown cases to set up estate administration and proper plaintiffs.

A great new member of our team in all three cases and representing his son's estate has been "investigator extraordinaire" Andy Pears. Notwithstanding, his own words and son's killing, this retired Air Force colonel is actually a gentle soul, with a kind, saintly heart and excellent mind.

The biggest problem encountered in all three cases was the "immunity" defense, either (a) sovereign immunity; (b) state action immunity; and/or (c) "qualified immunity."

The foundational immunity is called sovereign immunity. That defense clothes and protects from suit any state official acting in his official capacity. That includes a sheriff, under the law considered as much a state official as a governor, state attorney general, or state tax collector. Although a deputy sheriffs' domain is generally only one county wide, he is protected by sovereign immunity from all actions in his official capacity. This immunity does not extend to a county commissioner or county coroner.

The deputy sheriff is protected from liability if he arrests someone, because arresting is an official duty. However, a deputy sheriff is "not protected" if he does something out of personal gratification, such as grabbing a female for sexual gratification and kissing. In such an act, the sheriff is deemed to have acted in his "individual capacity" and has no protection from liability.

The sovereign immunity concept evolved from the Old English common law doctrine, "The King can do no wrong." If such immunity is found, it operates as an "absolute ban" to any liability claims.

Unfortunately, in the 1980s the 11th Circuit U.S. Court of Appeals, based in Atlanta and covering Georgia, Alabama, and Florida, started expanding this protection. This newly evolving protection from the U.S. Constitution was given the name "qualified immunity."

Most U.S. Constitutional law cases involve one of the following U.S. Constitutional rights:

First Amendment right to freedom of speech;

First Amendment right to freedom of political association;

Fourth Amendment right against unlawful search and seizure;

Fifth Amendment right against self-incrimination;

Sixth Amendment right to trial by jury;

Eighth Amendment right against cruel and unusual punishment;

Fourteenth Amendment right to due process and equal protection of the laws.

If a public official violates one of these rights, then he is not authorized to do so, he has done so in his individual capacity. This enables a plaintiff to get around the sovereign immunity defense or at least challenge the qualified immunity defense.

Frequently cited in the 1980s was 11th Circuit Judge J. L. Edmondson of Florida who said, "Rare is the day, these days, when a qualified immunity is not granted." The 11th Circuit includes cases from Alabama, Florida, and Georgia. The other ten circuits cover the other states. They are, collectively, the highest courts in the U.S. below the U. S. Supreme Court.

I remember bumping into U.S. District Judge U. W. Clemon at a Selma civil rights event in the 1990s. He was not on the bench at the time  and expansively bemoaned that "qualified immunity is destroying civil rights cases." From the 1980s through the current day, I have repeated his bemoaning. But "qualified" does not mean "absolute."

The 11th Circuit in the 2011 case of Castle v. Appalachian Tech. College, 631 F.3d 1194, 1197, stated:

> Courts should utilize a two-part framework to evaluate qualified immunity claims. The first element is whether the plaintiff's allegations, if true, establish a constitutional violation. The second element is whether the constitutional right at issue was clearly established at the time of the defendant's alleged misconduct. Both elements of this test must be present for an official to lose qualified immunity, and this two-pronged analysis may be done in whatever order is deemed most appropriate for the case.

If a plaintiff fails to establish either one, then the defendant is entitled to qualified immunity.

So how does this defense apply to the following three cases?

## JONATHAN PEARS

The killing of Jonathan Pears by the Elmore County deputies in late July 21, 2021, came after his mother's 911 call for mental health assistance. In our lawsuit his father, Andrew "Andy" Pears, sued as administrator of his son Jonathan's estate. Pears was also suing because of his own injuries caused by the Elmore County deputies. Shooting his son from 90 feet away was a bullying act by Deputy Jacob Boddie, one of four SWAT team members in body armor, who had marched through the woods, down a hill, adjacent to the Pears's family residence.

Boddie fired at least three gunshots. Each hit Jonathan Pears in his chest and killed him. Boddie could easily have used non-lethal weapons, like a Taser, a chemical spray agent, or bully club, but did not. Likewise, the deputies could have shot Jonathan in the legs, but did not.

One of the sheriff's deputies, standing near Jonathan's dying body, gave a false excuse to his mother, Mary Pierce, stating, "We had to shoot him; he came after your husband (Andy Pears) with a knife."

The truth was absolutely, totally, the opposite, and all the deputies should know it, whatever they may say. Live testimony and videotape show that Andy Pears was far removed from Jonathan at the time of the shooting, and Jonathan was not even approaching his father. Instead, the father was on his butt on grass at the bottom of a hill, handcuffed by deputy Arnold Oliver III, and nightmarishly witnessing the killing of his own son.

How outrageous can that be for a law enforcement officer to kill a decorated veteran of the Afghan war? Or anybody for that matter? It makes me sick. Yet, the deputy was seeking to escape accountability and liability, due to the anti-civil rights doctrine of "qualified immunity."

## TIDERA HARRIS

Tidera Harris was no Boy Scout. He was minding his own business when he came by the home of his children's mama, Chimeka Minnefield, to get his belongings. Harris had five children there, ranging in age from toddler to late teen, each with a variation on their father's name. Harris had committed no crime and had threatened no one. His children's mom had not called 911. Apparently, a busybody neighbor did. Two Montgomery police officers showed up, one a young Black female, Renee Hilton, the other a young Black male, Gregory Harvey. Both officers met Harris and Minnefield, who confirmed that Harris was packing up his belongings.

Officer Harvey asked Harris to talk with him outside, a request which Harris politely complied with, answering questions about his identity. As Harris went outside, police lady Hilton commented to officer Harvey, "he got keys," to which officer Harvey responded, "OK; he's good."

It was all peaceful and amicable in the small front yard until Harris answered his phone. He said "Hello," before walking away from Officer Harvey. At that point, Harvey said "Hey, hey no, hey dog" and then pulled out his gun. He fired two shots at Harris's back, from about 15 yards away.

The badly wounded Harris had committed no felony, and not even a misdemeanor. He was not under arrest and had been given no warning when he walked off.

There was simply no good excuse for this police shooting. For months, the City of Montgomery stonewalled my legal team and me, refusing to even acknowledge the shooting and failing to disclose the name of the police shooter. A letter to Montgomery Mayor Steven Reed went unanswered, despite the mayor's repeated statement about the city maintaining "transparency."

That left us with no alternative but to file suit. We did so in November 2021. Discovery demands eventually required the city to admit the shooting and name the two officers, including the shooter.

The city soon filed a petition to remove the case from state court to federal court. This was due to the U.S. Constitutional rights issues. Either court was okay with us. We drew U.S. District Judge Keith Watkins, a fair jurist.

Our First Amended Complaint was filed on May 20, 2022. We revealed the shooter's name for the first time at a news conference. At that time,

Harris was able to speak to the press. Channel 12 (NBC) did come, but the station would not run a story they said. They wanted to be fair to both sides, but the City of Montgomery continued to stonewall. Since the city would not comment, Channel 12 would not run the story. How unfair. How un-journalistic.

Meanwhile, the understaffed *Montgomery Advertiser* finally sent out an unseasoned college intern two weeks later. Her story was also stymied by the city's unwillingness to talk. Obviously, Montgomery is not Minneapolis where George Floyd was mistreated. You would think that historic Montgomery would have the ability to attract national press in a case like this. The *Advertiser* story, well written by intern Destini Ambus, was finally released as a front-page article on August 18, 2022, with a color photograph of Tidera Harris and the headline "He Just Shot Me, He Didn't Say Anything." Still no national press picked up on it.

Meanwhile, by late May 2022, Harris had had nine surgeries and incurred medical costs of more than $700,000. He is now paraplegic and in a wheelchair for life. Also, the Christopher Reeves Foundation estimated Harris will need $1.5 million of medical treatment annually in the future.

Through discovery, we eventually learned that the shooter, 23-year-old African American rookie Gregory Harvey, had been on the job for only seven months. This was his first shooting. The City of Montgomery either failed to train him adequately and/or negligently hired and trained him, given his significant prior drug history.

For the City of Montgomery to argue a "qualified immunity" defense in this case is absurd. It makes you sick. No wonder the city stonewalled, ashamed to admit its role in the still-developing case and unwilling to pay Harris for the damage its police officer caused.

## LARRY BROWN

Inmate Larry Brown was murdered at Bullock Correctional Facility, an Alabama prison in Union Springs in Bullock County, an hour southeast of Montgomery. This happened in April 2021, amidst institutional policies allowing the same.

It was heartbreaking to meet Myrna Brown, mother of prison inmate

Larry Brown, and his two sisters Jennifer Brown, and Deketa Brown-Brewer. They couldn't control their tears. Despite Brown's imprisonment, the family had stayed close.

They told the sad story of a total prison breakdown, with inmates running around like wild men looking for the next weak, vulnerable inmate to rape, rob, or beat to death. It was like a game. This all sounded unbelievable . . . until we started investigating the facts.

It was not always that bad at the Alabama Department of Corrections. In earlier years, the prisons were more sanely run. But these were the disastrous years of 2021 and 2022.

Larry Brown has been an inmate at the Bullock Correctional Facility for nine years before his death. From January 2021 to April 1, 2021, Brown and other inmates at Bullock repeatedly informed facility officers about the numerous deadly threats made upon Brown's life by other inmates. Thus, we alleged that the two wardens named as defendants and Alabama prison commissioner Jeffrey Dunn had "specific knowledge" about the substantial risk to Brown's life. Dunn failed to act to prevent Brown's death, despite a duty to do so, in violation of the Eighth Amendment.

The officials very much had a duty. It is well settled law that prison officials must "take reasonable measures to guarantee the safety of inmates," and the "prison officials violate the Eighth Amendment against cruel and unusual punishment, if the prison official is deliberately indifferent to the substantial risk of serious injury to an inmate who suffers injury." See Marbury v. Warden, 936 F.3d 1227 (11th Cir. 2019); Lane v. Philbin, 835 f.3d 1302, 1307 (11th Cir. 2016) as guiding precedential legal cases.

We filed our Second Amended Complaint on August 25, 2021. Our informal discovery gave us the names of six to seven inmates in the pack who bludgeoned Brown to death on April 2, 2021. Brown actually lingered on life support at Baptist Hospital, brain dead, until May 5, 2021.

We were excited to draw Myron Thompson as our judge. He appears to have a great conscience about inmates in Alabama prisons. The only problem was the federal court's overwhelming number of cases. Judge Thompson took a long time to rule. Like a year or more. Meanwhile evidence disappears, or is dissipated, or no longer lives.

Since formal discovery cannot officially begin until a motion to dismiss is denied, Judge Thompson took a year to rule on the defense motions to dismiss Commissioner Dunn and the two wardens. We filed several discovery motions seeking special opportunities to take depositions before witnesses disappeared. Unfortunately, Judge Thompson delayed ruling on these motions. His court finally issued a ruling in July 2022 that we had not shown "a particularized need" for the information.

The defendants all asserted the "qualified immunity defense." In case law, qualified immunity will protect defendants from ever having to engage in the "burdens of discovery."

The U.S. Supreme Court proclaimed in Farmer vs. Brennan, 511 U.S. 825, 842 (1994) that:

> To avoid this qualified immunity trap, a plaintiff must prove deliberate indifference which is, an Eighth Amendment violation. To do so, a plaintiff must show "that the official acted or failed to act despite his knowledge of a substantial risk of serious harm." Importantly, however, a plaintiff "need not show that a prison official acted, or failed to act, believing that harm actually would befall an inmate . . . "

As alleged in our Third Amended Complaint, there existed a history of widespread abuse putting Warden Jones and Warden Lamar on notice of the need to correct the alleged deprivation, and that he or she failed to do so that this custom or policy resulted in deliberate indifference to constitutional rights. These facts supported an inference that the wardens directed subordinates to act unlawfully or knew that subordinates would act unlawfully and failed to stop them from doing so.

I quote my partner David Sawyer's brief as follows:

> The Eleventh Circuit in Rodriguez v. Secretary for Dept. of Corrections, 508 F.3d 611 (11th Cir 2007), held the Eighth Amendment imposes a duty on prison officials "to protect prisoners from violence at the hands of other prisoners." . . .
>
> A prison official violates the 8th amendment when he actually

(subjectively) knows that an inmate is facing a substantial risk of serious, yet disregards that known risk by failing to respond to it in an (objectively) reasonable manner.

We think these strict legal standards are met by the facts of our deceased client Larry Brown. There are many state attorneys now working against us, some at great expense, including such top outside law firms as Maynard Cooper of Birmingham.

Given the slow wheels of discovery and all that is on Judge Thompson's plate, I couldn't know when we would get to bat. Meanwhile, we dealt with the slowly strangling defense of qualified immunity, not only in the three cases cited, but in attacks of many other civil rights victims.

## 22

# Arbitration Still a Bully

In this, my last about bullies, I would be remiss not to address one of the biggest bullies roaming around our country and society generally. This bully cheats consumers and intimidates victims. It is "involuntary arbitration," with all its ugliness. It is a continuing fiasco, a spider web often used to bully consumers and employees alike. Not to be confused with "voluntary arbitration" to speed a resolution along. Or "mediation," where both sides have the "right to walk away."

In my first book about the legal world, *The People's Lawyer*, there's a chapter entitled: "Ron Mays and the Arbitration Albatross." My second book, *Civil Rights in My Bones*, has a chapter entitled "Virginia College's Arbitration Noose."

Both chapters detail the gross unfairness inflicted upon innocent employees or consumers who are ripped off and denied the right to effectively do anything about it.

In 1995, Ron Mays, a very successful salesman of copier machines for Lanier Business Products, and a second cousin once removed of baseball great Willie Mays, came to see me. He claimed that new managers coming up from Florida and down from New Jersey to Alabama were encouraging an atmosphere of blatant racial discrimination and harassment at the Fortune 200 company where he worked.

It was in stark contrast to Mays's first year of employment where, under native Alabama management, he far exceeded his sales quotas. In fact, he was rewarded with plaques, honors, and a trip to the Caribbean. In some months, Mays sold more copiers than the other 12 employees combined—all of whom were white.

To say that the new managers got off on the wrong foot with Mays was a huge understatement.

These new managers started referring to Ron Mays as "blue gum" and "the brotherman." They made monkey-like sounds mocking Mays behind his back. They even threatened, in a joke considered funny by them but not by Mays, that they would make him "the target on a hunting trip."

When Mays filed a charge of racial discrimination with the EEOC, Lanier Company reacted by taking away much of Mays's geographical sales territory. We added a "wrongful retaliation" claim to our original EEOC charge. Given declining sales caused by his lesser territory and the cold and hostile working environment, Lanier fired Mays.

As fate would have it, we learned that, in 1994, when Mays first came to work for Lanier, he signed an employment agreement with an arbitration provision.

My law partner Kenneth Shinbaum, after doing research, concluded that Mays's prospects were bleak. If he contested the arbitration clause in court under existing laws, he would likely lose in the 11th Circuit Court of Appeals, after the passage of two years' time. So reluctantly, Mays and associate attorney Karen Sampson and I proceeded to arbitration and hoped for the best.

As quoted from *The People's Lawyer*:

> Their hopes were dashed pretty quickly. To begin arbitration, Mays had to pay the American Arbitration Association a filing fee of $3,600. (In federal court, the filing fee would have been only $150). Moreover, the daily bill of $2,000 for the arbitrators was split between Mays and Lanier. The prospect of paying $1,000 a day out of pocket was understandably daunting to Mays, but he was assured the case would probably be finished in two days.

Instead, the Atlanta attorney representing Lanier stretched the trial out to nine days and kept Mays on the witness stand for four days, cross-examining him about matters that happened 15 years earlier. Over my objections, the Arbitrator allowed it to continue, even though the questions involved irrelevant matters designed to run up the lawyer's bill and tax Mays half of the Arbitrator's time expense at a hefty rate.

I objected continuously. However, the Arbitrator's reply was "we'll give it the weight we think it deserves." The Arbitrator didn't prohibit irrelevant questions. He handled evidentiary matters the fairer way a federal judge would have. It was obviously in the Arbitrator's financial interest to keep the proceedings going.

By the time the hearing ended, Ron Mays owed the American Arbitration Association an initial $12,600. Then, the Atlanta attorney requested briefs based on transcripts of the hearing. The arbitrator complied, at the cost to Mays of an additional $8,500. By the time travel expenses for out-of-state witnesses and other discovery calls were added, Mays ended up owing some $23,000—win, lose, or draw. Not surprisingly, the Arbitrator, knowing who was much more likely to come back to him again for more business in the future, and who could easily pay his bill, ruled against Mays.

The latter case of "Virginia College's Arbitration Noose" was just as bad. Naive students got suckered into Virginia College's "spider web." As stated in *Civil Rights in My Bones*, "Being lyrically blunt, arbitration causes an employee, consumer, or student to be used, bruised, contused, and abused."

Finally, in the past year, the U.S. Congress, due to much pressure from employees sexually harassed, created a legislative exception, allowing such victims to declare null and void arbitration clauses in such victimizations. This badly needs to be extended to all arbitration.

I never thought it could happen, but it did in early 2022, when a new client Donna Gable, the former executive director of the Alexander City Housing Authority, came to see me. I found myself insisting that an arbitration clause in a "Handbook for Employees of the Housing Authority" was inapplicable to Gable, because, as executive director, she was an "employee-at-will," and thus not entitled to a hearing.

My partner Kenneth Shinbaum and I drafted a lawsuit for the Tallapoosa County Circuit Court as leverage. We insisted upon the right to an arbitration hearing, as opposed to no rights at all for an employee-at-will. Finally, the Alexander City Housing Authority caved in, and gave us a hearing on August 3–4, 2022, before a "supposedly independent" arbitrator, with fees and costs to be shared equally.

The arbitrator Allen Schreiber was surprisingly fair in the way he ran the hearing, but not surprisingly, he ruled against us on the ground that Gable was in fact an employee-at-will. Like the other arbitrator, this one knew he would be called again by the Alexander City Housing Authority. He knows it would be unlikely to ever be called by Donna Gabel.

Legislators with a conscience and government executives must work together, in my humble opinion, to rid society of this grossly unfair "Arbitration bully" against fairness, justice, and American democracy.

## 23

# Anti-Semitism Unrestrained

Is anti-Semitism still alive and well in America today? In Alabama? I would like to think not. Most regrettably, it occasionally rears its ugly head. Two of my own human angels on earth are Jewish. They are my own personal attorney, Bobby Segall, and my law partner, Kenneth Shinbaum.

I consider myself part Jewish because a DNA test says I am two percent Ashkenazi Jew. An Irish, Scottish, English, French, and Spanish heritage is also mine. I take my Christian faith seriously. I know that Jesus and the First Century Christian disciples were all Jewish. Beyond that, I know the Old Testament comes from the Jewish Torah, the Old Testament foundation of Christianity.

What drives modern-day anti-Semitism? There have been World War II atrocities against Jews. There have been attacks against synagogues in America. For individual Jews, this remains a thorny problem. Modern-day Israel and its friends safeguard our Jewish brethren.

I am not surprised that Robert Hadley, a 43-year-old Jew both ethnically and religiously, still practices his faith. He drove up from Andalusia to see me about the ugly anti-Semitism he experienced at his Coffee County Commission job in Enterprise. The basic facts are alleged in a charge first filed with the Equal Employment Opportunity Commission in Birmingham, followed by a federal lawsuit in Montgomery.

In September 2014, Hadley was hired by the Coffee County Commission as an electrician. From there, he worked his way up the ranks and became Assistant Maintenance Superintendent. Robert has also maintained a spotless employment record. He has never received any disciplinary notices. He has never been written up for incompetence or negligent performance. He has always been an exemplary employee. He also produces an excellent quality of work.

Unfortunately, in 2015, Hadley was increasingly a target of anti-Semitic comments and slurs by his co-employees of the Coffee County Commission. Anti-Semitic videos were played directly in his face, with an obvious intention of insulting him. Hadley was on one occasion asked, "Why are you working here? You know that all Jews are rich." Another employee at the landfill shop spouted out that the KKK will rise up and take back Washington from the Jews. Hadley reported these incidents to his supervisor Todd Rugg. Unfortunately, nothing was ever done to curb his anti-Semitic slurs.

On October 16, 2018, Chell Thomas, a janitor working under Hadley, asked him if he believed in Jesus. Hadley responded that he was Jewish. Thomas responded, "I can't work for you then. You're going to hell." Surprised, Hadley reported this to his supervisor Todd Ruggs. Unfortunately, nothing was ever done to correct the anti-Semitic digs and slurs.

On November 26, 2018, Hadley met with Marty Lentz, County Engineer, and informed him he had been passed over for a promotion. Hadley responded he had not received a fair evaluation. Unfortunately, as Superintendent Todd Ruggs and Supervisor Ron Scroggins wrongfully gave him bad reviews, which flowed out of their own negative feelings toward Jews. Hadley proclaimed that Ruggs and Scroggins "flashed white supremacy tattoos around the workplace." Incredibly both later denied the racial interpretation. Their tattoos were hard to miss, since they were on their hands, arms, and neck. To Hadley these were symbols of racism.

On that same November 26, Hadley reminded Lentz he was Jewish and complained about bias he was encountering. Lentz replied that he was talking with someone about Hadley being Jewish. When Hadley inquired about who that might be, Lentz evaded the question.

On April 29, 2019, Lentz called Hadley back into his office. He asked him if he had purchased a spray paint gun. Hadley had in fact done so for a paint job at the commission. Supervisor Scroggins accused Hadley of falsifying his time sheet. Hadley responded that the spray paint gun was obtained in accordance with commission rules, but that he had never falsified any time sheet.

In a Hobson's choice, Lentz offered Hadley two different letters the

Coffee County Commission had prepared for him to sign. One was a resignation letter, the other a termination letter. Lentz informed Hadley that he must resign, to receive unemployment compensation. But if he refused, he must be terminated, and the commission would fight his unemployment. Given the pervasively cold and hostile anti-Semitism towards Hadley and his Jewish faith, he resigned under the pressure. As the plaintiff's attorney, I know this is "a constructive discharge," leading to Hadley asserting his legal rights.

An EEOC "right-to-sue" suit was obtained, with a suit filed in September 2020. Depositions soon began. With assistance of associate attorney, Chase Estes, present for Hadley's deposition, I took depositions of the Coffee County leaders. Subsequently, the defendant's attorney, Jamie Frawley, filed a motion for summary judgment.

Judge Emily Marks took her usual time in issuing a final Memorandum and Opinion on May 2, 2022. She granted summary judgment for the Coffee County Commission against Hadley, tossing him out of court.

Surprise, no surprise. Judge Marks dodged the anti-Jewish discrimination issue. She gave an esoteric, technical opinion, ruling that the "right-to-sue" issued by the EEOC (Equal Employment Opportunity Commission) was not good enough. Instead, Judge Marks ruled we needed one more "right-to-sue" from the U.S. Justice Department, because the Coffee County Commission was a governmental entity.

I was livid and my client was deeply disturbed. That is an enormous understatement. Not to have the merits of one's claim heard is vastly unfair. I quickly countered with a "FRCP Rule 59 motion to alter or amend the judgment, or in the alternative, an FRCP Rule 60 motion for relief from judgment." I attached an affidavit stating:

> I have been a practicing attorney in Montgomery, Alabama for the last 47 years (or since April 1975) and before that, I practiced law in New York, where I graduated from Columbia Law School in 1971.
>
> It would not be an overstatement to say that I have handled at least 200 or more charges of unlawful employment discrimination with the Equal Employment Opportunity Commission in Birmingham, Alabama. I have

always been informed by the EEOC that all I need to file suit was right-to-sue from the EEOC.

This includes many EEOC complaints and rights-to-sue obtained from the EEOC on other respondent cases that included public entities such as Auburn University, the City of Montgomery, the City of Selma, and the City of Wetumpka, etc. None of these rights-to-sue included any language that I also needed a right-to-sue from the U.S. Justice Department to file suit.

Attached hereto is the dismissal and right-to-sue issued to Mr. Robert Hadley, the Plaintiff in the case for which this affidavit is issued. As you can see, there is nothing in this Notice of Right-to-Sue that requires anyone, including me, or my client, Mr. Robert Hadley, to get permission from the U.S. Justice Department. See attached exhibit.

I can also recall a few cases in the past in which the EEOC has forwarded a claim to the U.S. Department of Justice. However, in such cases, the Justice Department approval was received, well beyond a six-month period, if ever a response was received. In many instances, we still pursued a case with only a Right-to-Sue from the EEOC, and with nothing heard back from the Justice Department. In fact, the EEOC had a rule that if it didn't make a finding within six months, it would automatically issue a right-to-sue.

I also attached the EEOC's right-to-sue issued on August 5, 2020. Nothing said therein said we needed a Justice Department's right-to-sue. Further, in my experience in the past, with the EEOC. I checked with the Justice Department on cases involving governmental entities. So, why did plaintiff Hadley and I have to duplicate that to obtain a second piece of paper?

I didn't stop there. On June 9, 2022, a letter was sent to Bradley Anderson, the director of the EEOC in Birmingham. He was quite upset with the federal court in Montgomery and promised to help all he could. He agreed that my EEOC right-to-sue should be more than adequate.

Unfortunately, Judge Marks denied my motion on May 4, 2022. Armed with a helpful letter from director Anderson, I strongly contended to the court that the EEOC had earlier "dismissed" the charge. Thus, no right-to-sue was needed from the Justice Department. Anderson added that the EEOC could issue a right-to-sue, pursuant to 29 C.F.R. § 1601.28(d). If no dismissal had been issued by the EEOC, a second right-to-sue from the Justice Department could be obtained, he added.

To encourage the court to have a sense of moral urgency about the anti-Semitic issue, I added:

> This Honorable Court should take judicial notice that lately, in America, a virulent form of anti-Semitism or anti-Jewish prejudice has been re-emerging, raising its ugly head in America, and unfortunately, worldwide. At a synagogue in Pittsburg, within the last two years, an attack was launched by an extremist that actually killed several people. More recently, just weeks ago, a Rabbi and certain 15 members of a synagogue in Texas were held hostage under the threat of death by a gunman, until rescued. Similar incidents have occurred in other parts of the world. If courts of law, especially federal ones where evidence of such anti-Semitism bias exists do not take a stand, history is doomed to repeat itself. It is unimaginable that another Auschwitz could occur, especially in our great country. To cut anti-Semitism off at its roots is imperative. This case represents such an opportunity.

Unbelievably, notwithstanding EEOC Director Anderson's clarification that our right-to-sue was good, Judge Marks again denied it. She added that the court could have issued an equitable waiver. However, she would not do so. She insisted a separate right-to-sue from the Justice Department must be obtained. Her opinion of June 29, 2022, mocked our anti-Semitism claim. She stated in her lead paragraph: "This is not a case about 'another Auschwitz[.]' (Doc 45 at 15) Nor is it about 'mass shootings' 'happening almost daily[.]' (Doc 60 at 3) It is a case about alleged discrimination in the workplace."

So, what did we do? We telephoned and wrote to the Justice Department, and I obtained a Justice Department right-to-sue a few weeks later. In fact, the EEOC and the Justice Department assisted me. So, I filed a third motion to alter or amend the decision. This time I attached the sacred Justice Department's letter, which gave me 90 days from the July 25, 2022, receipt of the right-to-sue, to pursue the claim.

Problem solved? Let's wait and see.

This highly coveted Justice Department's right-to-sue should have automatically "healed" our lawsuit. I attached it to a third motion of July 25, 2022. You'd think Judge Marks would have given me another 90 days.

The court should have automatically granted my motion. But 30 days passed, and then 60 days, with no ruling from our judge. I was afraid the court was sitting on my motion, and afraid she was going to let the 90 days run. I learned the court might rule against us.

As time passed, I was getting worried. I saw Judge Marks at a federal court social gathering for judges and attorneys in late September. She greeted me with a smile. However, I became even more concerned, and knew well that appearances can be misleading.

I called Judge Marks's law clerk the next day and explained my concern about 90 days being close to running, and asked when a ruling might be. The judge was "working on it" the clerk replied.

The next day, we were given a ruling. Against all rationale, and against what the court had earlier said, Judge Marks unbelievably ruled against us a third time. I patiently tried to control my emotions and called my client. I also consulted with other attorneys in and outside the firm. We concluded we had but two possibilities. One was to appeal her ruling to the 11th Circuit. The problem we had was that if we won, Judge Marks would remain on the case and likely rule against us again. We had completely lost confidence in this judge's ability to treat us fairly in this case. Thus, my client decided not to appeal. In return, the opposition agreed not to file a Bill of Costs against my client. This saved us several thousand dollars.

Our other alternative was to file a brand-new lawsuit, on or before the Justice Department's 90-day expiration (Oct. 23, 2022). Law partner David Sawyer's research concluded that we would likely run into the res judicata defense, meaning the case had "already been decided." Thus, our new case would be dismissed.

It is risky for me to write this chapter, as I am openly doing here. The

First Amendment's right to freedom of speech should protect me in what I have said here. Ironically, Judge Marks's father, Charles Coody, as a lower magistrate judge, had ruled in my favor on a First Amendment case only four years earlier.

I add in the court's defense and mine, that I greatly respect the office that Judge Marks holds. I do not criticize her morality or ethics, but I am highly critical of her judicial philosophy. She is "the most pro-status quo and anti-plaintiff" of all the many federal judges I have ever known. See Chapter 20 about her anti-plaintiff rulings. She was in three age discrimination cases I've had with her in the last several years.

I hate to mention this, but I wonder. About 15 years ago, when Emily Marks was a private attorney just like me, she filed a bar complaint against me in a case, saying I had wrongfully said her witnesses were "embellishing" their testimony. "How dare he do that," she complained to the Alabama Bar. The Bar later informed me that it was a "frivolous complaint." As such, the Bar didn't ask me to respond, dismissing her complaint.

I brace myself to see what kind of complaint Judge Marks may file against me in retaliation for what I have written in this chapter. I trust the U.S. Constitution will protect my Freedom of Speech rights on this issue of public concern.

Lost in all this hullabaloo is that the anti-Semitic, anti-Jewish discrimination which my client Robert Hadley suffered once again goes unrestrained, and unchecked. To that extent justice was denied. Robert Hadley was bullied in more ways than one.

# Alabama Prisons—the Biggest Bully of Them All

The biggest bully by far in Alabama is the torture chamber. Alabama prisons are hell holes for both inmates and correctional officers, given all the knives and rocks spread across the grounds.

It is totally embarrassing. It is very deadly and a national and international scandal tarnishing both Alabama and the U.S.A. and Alabama's highest authorities, including Governor Kay Ivey. The Alabama legislature has tolerated and allowed inmates to carry weapons. The wardens are unable to stop it. Drugs remain rampant and easily available. There is a scandalous shortcoming of correctional officers. It is difficult to control the inmates' access to drugs.

If a correctional officer fails to jump in like "Superman" and break up another correctional officer's striking inmates, then the officer may be indicted by a federal grand jury for violating civil rights. He ends up spending years as a federal inmate.

Alabama prisons have always been bad. My book *Only in Alabama* has a chapter entitled "Alabama Prisons a Nightmare."

Unfortunately, prison conditions became worse, but much worse during the Covid years, 2020–2022. Inmates have died in record numbers. The worst Alabama prisons are Bullock Correctional Facility located in Union Springs, southeast of Montgomery, and Donaldson Correctional Facility located in Bessemer, west of Birmingham.

The severity of prison conditions must give crazies in Russia, Iran, China, and elsewhere much finger-pointing material towards our beloved America.

When I wrote this chapter in October 2022, I had two wrongful death suits against the commissioner of ADOC and wardens in Bullock, based on the pathetic killing of inmates. One involves Larry Brown, bludgeoned by mentally ill inmates in April 2021. A new young female correctional officer stood by. She was too afraid to jump in, concerned that she might be killed herself. She probably would have been.

The second case involved Lawrence Turner. He was stabbed to death at the Bullock Correctional Facility in July 2022. We're contemplating a third wrongful death case in the same prison. There have been many more, especially state-wide. It frequently takes a year to get a federal judge to rule on a simple motion to dismiss, necessary before discovery can begin.

The U.S. Justice Department initiated a major suit against the Alabama Department of Corrections in 2020. It was about overworking, violence, and the high risk of death for inmates. There is an encyclopedia of brutality in all 14 of the state's prisons. Despite added scrutiny from outside, conditions only get worse. The counter-productive federal strategy of prosecuting so many inmates has backfired.

The slow wheels of justice continue to turn at a snail's pace. The battle between the Feds and the state will take years to wind on.

Every day I get emails from Jennifer Brown, the sister and administratrix of her deceased brother Larry Brown's estate. Another client, Fred Turner, the administrator of his brother Lawrence's estate, is also incensed about the brutal and unnecessary death of his brother.

What both are saying is that their brothers were very wrongfully murdered in prisons. These murders could have been prevented with adequate resources and more enlightened leadership.

The *Montgomery Advertiser* and the *Birmingham News* have run front-page exposés. On Friday, October 2, 2022, the *Advertiser*'s headline, in big bold letters, read "A PRISON SYSTEM IN DISARRAY," reporting on a statewide labor strike by inmates. There have also been hunger strikes.

Carla Crower, the Executive Director of the Alabama Appleseed, reported, "What we saw in the video is outrageous, but it's been outrageous in DOC for so long, and it just doesn't let up. It is not unusual to have multiple homicides or drug overdoses in a week, and videos circulating of sleeping guards and open-air drug use in the dorms. That is the new normal."

Meanwhile, on the same front page is the headline "State seeks second execution date of Alan Miller." The state prisons have frequently botched these brutal executions.

The federal government wants to do something about it. Its lawsuit is a correct step. However, its often wrongful prosecution of correctional officers has back-fired, substantially reducing the number of job seekers applying for correctional officer positions.

On September 26, 2022, inmates state-wide launched a labor strike. Five days later Governor Ivey, from the comfort of her Governor's Mansion, pooh-poohed the strike. She said the State Department of Corrections had things well under control. The *Montgomery Advertiser* said, "Images and interviews from inside the state's prisons show a system in disarray, with deteriorating conditions, pervasive violence, multiple deaths and stabbings, many seen on video."

Ivey responded that, "Everything's still operational . . . there's no disruption in essential services." The truth was that at least five of the state's prisons were shut down by the strike.

Ivey continues to bury her head in the sand like an ostrich. All the violence, corruption, and deaths are bad forms of bullying, aided and abetted by the commissioner of the Alabama Department of Corrections. Judge David Proctor of the U.S. District Court for the Northern District of Alabama instructed counsel to be ready for trial in November 2024.

## 25

# Wrapping It Up

I don't pretend that this book will be popular. Criticism is a risk worth assuming, and speaking out against the Establishment's wrongdoings is risky, but worthwhile and often necessary. Some call it "speaking truth to power." This can be done with civility, diplomacy, and even kindness on occasion, and works best when done so.

After 51 years as an attorney, and 77 years of living, I am often short on time. Better to publish my thoughts while I can.

Sometimes books have legs, as with my sparsely promoted book about the French Resistance, *From Vacillation to Resolve*, written in 1968 as a college thesis, but only published 50 years later in 2018. Somehow its legs ran up to New York, and then to Paris. In 2019, it was nominated for a top French book award, the "American Library in Paris" book award. My local publishers were astounded, and so was I. Nothing was ever said in Montgomery media about this international recognition.

I do enjoy writing. Most good authors draw from their own experiences. I am no exception. Mine is from the rich ore of my own legal work, involved with helping people struggling with bullies. Such work is my hobby.

This final book was begun in early July 2022 from the cabin room Leslie and I were sharing on a ferryboat cruise up the western Greenlandic coast in the Arctic Ocean. Some of the scenery was absolutely breathtaking, some not. My dear wife and I were virtually the only Americans of 200 aboard this ship. We greatly enjoyed all the Europeans and native Greenlanders. We enjoy world traveling, another hobby. Our journeys have been sandwiched intermittently between fifty years of lawyering. That includes an enjoyably active family life now with three married adult children and seven grands.

I have experienced my share of knocks and bruises. A huge part of life is learning how to "roll with the punches," and "keep on keeping on." Both lawyers and writers require perseverance. Both endeavors are actually fun in my life's work, allowing me to draw on a deep theological reservoir developed over many years. I am enormously indebted to my awesome wife Leslie, given her continued support and encouragement.

I hope the readers of this book will have learned something. These true-life stories, together with my analysis of bullying, involve the predicaments of life.

I hope to encourage people to stand up to the bullies in their lives. That sometimes involves fighting back—metaphorically, not physically. Everyone has a right to defend oneself if attacked. That must be done carefully, and it is always best to avoid a physical confrontation. A smile, a chuckle, or a kind word are much better than a threat or self-defensive assault with a weapon.

I must be careful to qualify that last remark. It leads to another sensitivity of mine, the proliferation and misuse of guns. Except in extreme situations, no one should take up a weapon and hurt someone. It can easily get one charged with assault, manslaughter, or even murder. At our law firm, we have had good citizen clients come to us. They face such consequences, even if they were acting in self-defense.

A diplomatic resolution saves lives and can keep one out of prison. So I tell clients to "stay away from guns and knives" and avoid getting oneself shot or stabbed. In hand-to-hand combat, I, as a former wrestling champion, could handle myself well, even at my age. But too many people carry guns to kill. Please avoid inciting someone, especially with a gun.

It is sad that social media has enabled family and friends to stay in contact at little cost. This has also given rise to too many hostile users. Hot-button political issues include abortion, gun rights, and proper law enforcement parameters. These issues abound, dividing families and friends. Political correctness abuse exists equally on both the left and right. This sometimes foments bullies.

This leads me to my most major point. Stay in good touch with God, as Creator, Redeemer, and Sustainer, or all three. You can be Protestant,

Catholic, Jew, Orthodox, or even a non-believer. A true relationship with Jesus Christ as Lord usually leads to compassion. It involves a greater kindness towards others via the Great Commandment: one must love one's neighbor as oneself. If you truly love your neighbor, you will reap much better consequences. This includes better health as well as longer life.

I continue to aim for a high number of years and good health, increasingly aware that a devoted relationship with God, through faith and prayer, involves serving others, which is essential. My exercise and a good diet make for a happy relationship with my spouse and family. This contributes to longevity. Being grounded in the solid rock of a loving relationship with God is foundational to joy and peace. It is a better pathway to life with our Maker, in the eternal realm.

No one knows how many years we have left. Leslie and I look forward to growing closer to God and humankind. Thus we will better enjoy life on earth until we graduate to our eternal home.

# 26

# Depression Is a Bully

I wrote most of this book before October 1, 2022. At that time, I was feeling very good about everything.

I was born in Birmingham, grew up in Sewanee, Tennessee, attended the Sewanee Military Academy, applied to Princeton University, was accepted in 1964, and graduated in 1968. I applied to Columbia Law School and was accepted, attended from 1968–1971, and graduated in 1971.

I applied to and worked at a leading Wall Street law firm, Davis, Polk, and Wardwell. While living and working in New York City, I was invited to a party up on 86th Street on the East Side where I met my future bride, Leslie Burton, who had grown up in Brazil. We were engaged on December 28, 1973, and I introduced her to my parents in Alabama. She thought Alabama was much like Brazil. I told her, yes, both are Banana Republics, and she should be comfortable there.

I brought Leslie back to New York where she continued to work at Chemical Bank, but I began a new phase of my legal career, also on Wall Street. A good friend of mine, Tim Smith, also a graduate of Princeton and Columbia Law, persuaded me to accept an offer from American Express Company, and we enjoyed a good career together there in New York from 1973–75.

Leslie and I had enjoyed a first honeymoon, traveling around Norway, Sweden, Finland, and Russia. We enjoyed a second honeymoon in 1975, and traveled to Egypt, Kenya, South America, Angola, and Brazil. Upon our return to America, I accepted a new job at the Alabama Attorney General's Office and prosecuted white-collar crime as an assistant attorney general.

While in Rio de Janeiro, I had encountered a less-than-satisfactory decision. Leslie's parents decided to send her to Switzerland to study, which she did for two years before returning home to help me with my legal work, and then raise a family, including two daughters, Rachel and Grace, and a son, David. We were highly surprised by the circumstances of David coming to us. He appeared to have special gifts, including the gift of healing prayer among other charismatic talents. David's original coming was due first to advice we received from a world-class healing evangelist, Mahesh Chavda. He was married to another, highly annointed person, Bonnie, the mother of four children, Ben, Anna, Sarah, and Aaron. We visited Mahesh frequently from the 1980s into the 2000s. Mahesh came to Montgomery in 1994, 1996, 1997, and 2003.

Amazing miracles inspired us all to go into the healing Spirit, which is, of course, the Holy Spirit. We became increasingly excited and received many opportunities to further our interest in this gift. We did pursue the gift and were surprised at the results. This included one young girl only two years old and born blind. When she was brought forward for a healing prayer from Mahesh, she received a special touch of the Holy Spirit and fell backward into the arms of her mother and grandparents, Forest and Nancy Mobley, who were astonished that their granddaughter had received an almost complete healing from her blindness. So astonished as they were, gifted in the healing ministry to a lesser degree than Mahesh, they increased their zeal, and spread the word to others, who also became more excited about the power of the Spirit to still heal people in this day and age, much as was done in Jesus's time and subsequent times.

This ministry also inspired Leslie and me, and we sought further opportunities and received joyously those opportunities to pursue the ministry, too.

After returning to Alabama in 1975, Leslie and I attended Montgomery's Episcopal Church of the Ascension, but often on weekends traveled up to Pell City, 30 miles past Birmingham, to worship with my father, the Reverend Julian L. McPhillips Sr., and continue in the healing ministry, which he had long pursued as well with excellent results, especially with people, some of his church people, mentors, and others, some who were church members and others who were not.

Leslie and I were happy for a more charismatic Episcopal Church and thus we were among the leaders in founding a new Episcopal church named Christ The Redeemer, located in east Montgomery. As a founder, I helped lead the church into other healing and charismatic opportunities, and the church took off like a rocket in helping others.

Along the way, I encountered many people who experienced depression, which led me to explore this type of ministry too. I soon learned that about 90 percent of the country at one time or another had also experienced depression. I learned in 2004 that I was no exception, when I experienced a most unfortunate depression myself. Leslie, ever loyal, gave me her life support, and soon we were part of such a ministry, with her, always my better half, pursuing this ministry too.

I struggled from April to August that year with this depression. My daughter Rachel's wedding seemed to be the catalyst for my recovery. I walked her down the aisle and gave her away to a distinguished new son-in-law, Julius "Jay" Plucker V. By August, with the prayerful support of others, I soon recovered. During this time, I lost about 40 pounds, from 220 to 180, but after recovering I soon returned to my former weight. Others involved in praying for me included my father's former professor at the University of the South's School of Ministry in Sewanee, Tennessee, Art and Ellen Sanborn, the uncle and aunt of my son-in-law Corbett Lunsford. My recovery soon became complete, much to my great delight.

In 2022, I was suddenly hit by a second depression, much to my dismay, which began around October of that year. This depression in some ways hit harder and lasted until December of that year.

By January 2023, Leslie and I went to Atlanta where she was receiving treatment for cervical cancer. I received continued encouragement in my recovery by taking courses at the Emory University medical facilities. Much to my continued delight, soon we were both doing much better.

Before the second depression, I had begun writing this, my fourth book on the legal world. That is how and why my daughter Grace urged me to add to this book, already tentatively completed. Given my own depression experiences, I thought it was an excellent idea, and thus by August 2023, I started this addition to my original book of 25 chapters.

I can now see how the experience I have had is all too common, and we must learn to support one another better, too, as a part of the fabric of our life. Better mental health care is needed for people in the local and nationwide circles. Having experienced my share of this unfortunate malady, I wanted to relate some of what happened to me this second time from October to December 2022.

It all started when I became overwhelmed by having too many cases to handle simultaneously, at times almost 150. Too many. By the end of 2022, I decided it was time to retire to better cope with this depression and help my wife with her cancer as well. We thus started receiving treatments in Montgomery and Atlanta.

I want to share some of this experience with you.

We arrived in Atlanta, Leslie started receiving treatment, and I joined her in being treated because of the second depression. Soon we both were improving. Leslie kept getting better, and soon, so did I. We frequently consulted doctors and cooperated with each other in working with the medical community. Our children, of course, were frequently calling us. We were bolstered by prayer from friends and all of our family.

Our daughter Grace, whom we call "Amazing Grace," led our other children, Rachel, the older sister, and brother David in trips to see us in Atlanta, with David coming from Montgomery and Rachel from Germany (having recently moved from Huntsville), despite the great distance.

Over the years, I've too frequently noticed people experiencing depression who needed great help in dealing with their mental health problems. Grace, Rachel, and David were glad to help, and we were happy to receive their help and greatly benefited from their help.

Now that I've told you, I am much more at ease in talking about the depression I have experienced. I have learned much from sharing my story with others at the Subaru facility where Leslie and I have had our vehicles serviced for many years. This and other interactions helped us maintain a proper frame of mind, and avoid any further depression by me, Leslie, and others we know. These grateful friends have spread the word as best they can.

We love our friends, but we have come to recognize the true bully that depression is. We continue to meet people with depression and take every opportunity to assist these people in dealing with this bully. Leslie and I to share with friends and neighbors what to do with depression and what we have learned from our experiences. No greater duty exists for all mankind than to help our fellow man and woman when they are down and out, as in depression.

I have listened to many clients struggling with this bully. I have concluded that we must always strive to help everyone, as a duty back to our creator God.

I urge everyone to get involved and stand up to bullies, and depression is one of the greatest. I now leave this subject and trust and hope everyone will help not only the mentally ill but the average, ordinary person caught up in the pressures of life.

Amen.

# 27

# My Life Story

It began with my birth in Birmingham on November 13, 1946. I grew up in Cullman from 1946–1959.

I was rambunctious and tireless as a toddler. I once told a boogieman at two years old that I was not scared of him. I believed he was truly Santa Claus.

My earliest years consisted of bravado and mischief.

Other kids in the neighborhood couldn't believe the way I hit balls out of the park, which sometimes was just our family's backyard.

I was precocious as a youngster. It began with the first grade, where I was bigger and older than the others who had just started school.

By the time I hit the 6th grade, a decision was made to double-promote me to the 7th grade.

My next-door neighbor was Don Weaver, my little league battery mate was John Shaw, and my oldest friend from childhood was Courtney McKoy. We were all born in 1946. Don was the oldest born in February, John was born in August, Courtney in September, and I in November.

Stay tuned!

I attended my high school years at Sewanee Military Academy from 1959–1964. I graduated No. 2 in my class. I was accepted at Princeton, Duke, and the University of the South but chose Princeton.

After Princeton, I attended law school at Columbia University School of Law. I was fortunate to be elected chairman of the Law School Senate, equivalent to president of the student body.

Wrestling was my favorite sport. After winning two Ivy League Championships, I was accepted by the New York Athletic Club's team and won the Eastern AAU Championship in the 220-pound weight class, which was often combined with the Heavyweight class, leaving me sometimes at a disadvantage of 50–60 pounds.

I was on Wall Street as a lawyer from 1971–1975. Halfway through those years, I met thel ove of my life. Her name was J. Leslie Burton, with the same initials as me—JLM—after we married and she had the name J. Leslie McPhillips.

We were married on June 22, 1973, and honeymooned in Norway, Sweden, Finland, and Russia.

We returned to Alabama in 1975, but before we did, we took off on a second honeymoon, aided by discount travel costs from American Express, my last employer on Wall Street.

In that second honeymoon, we traveled to Egypt, Kenya, Tanzania, South Africa, and briefly Angola, before returning through Brazil, Leslie's native country. It was there I learned I had passed the Alabama Bar Exam on the first crack, after studying hard for six days at my parents' Lake Logan Martin home.

I specialized in white-collar crime prosecution. It was natural to become involved in civil rights. My interest in the subject was motivated by the Montgomery Bus Boycott in 1956, the Freedom Rides of 1961–1962, led by the heroic Dr. Fred Shuttlesworth, and the bombing of the Sixteenth Street Baptist Church in 1963. However, I will always remember the names McNair, (Chris's daughter), Collins, Roberts, and Wesley—the last names of the four precious young females killed in that infamous church bombing.

The lesson we learned from the civil rights movement is that hope and purpose grow out of chaos and destruction.

In subsequent years, I was assigned the job of pursuing white-collar crime and civil rights became my true mission in life.

Among my top assignments by Alabama Attorney General Bill Baxley (then very young, elected at age 28) was a civil lawsuit against real estate magnate Ed Lowder for self-dealing to himself the best properties in his job with the Alabama Farm Bureau (now known as ALFA).

Other accomplishments in my career include obtaining a judgment based on constitutional grounds against Montgomery police officers who unmercifully beat up vagrants, mostly black, who had no identification papers in their possession. Another type of civil rights case was a victory in a race discrimination class action against what is now the Alabama Department of Transportation.

Other notable cases included a victory in 1983 in Scottsboro in the famous case of Charlotte Payne versus Nationwide Insurance Company and another involving the Montgomery Police. In the Payne case, there was a desk from the Warm Springs, Georgia, estate of Franklin Delano Roosevelt, both pictures taken on the 60th birthdays of FDR and Eleanor Roosevelt.

As I progressed as an attorney, I ran unsuccessfully for the office of Attorney General of Alabama, seeking to follow in the footsteps of Bill Baxley, who brought me back to Alabama as an assistant attorney general in 1975. Another unsuccessful campaign in 2002 for a U.S. Senate seat further inspired me in my civil rights purpose, demonstrated over 47 years from 1975 to 2022.

Further development in my career included working on police brutality, and employment discrimination cases (race, sex, age, and disability).

As I continued my progress, I encountered depression on two different dates, the first from April to August 2006, and the second from October 2022 to March 2023.

I learned from these two depressions how to "roll with the punches." I did so by ample exercise, good food, fellowship and prayer, and church attendance.

As I now write this account, I have concluded that good physical and mental health are essential to good purpose, as is a strong relationship with the Lord. I encourage others to pursue this same Spirit and call upon one another, for better results, Amen.

## POSTSCRIPT

Afterward, my law firm grew and grew. Soon I encountered cases that required much more assistance. I also had a family that was needy, and not enough assistance from the office. I therefore turned to my office staff, and they responded in a big way I could not foresee. I therefore decided I needed to retire. The cases were coming in much too quickly. My brother

Frank had retired when he was eight years younger than when I made the decision.

I am now enjoying my retirement. Still in love with my wife Leslie as much as I ever was. She and my children and grandchildren are still the thrill of my life.

JULIAN L. McPHILLIPS, SEPTEMBER 15, 2023.

~